The Power of a Virtuous Woman

ALSO BY PAULA PENN-NABRIT

Morning By Morning:
How We Home-Schooled Our African-American Sons to the Ivy League

Exploring a New Synthesis:
Business Ethics & Diversity

As For Me and My House

Sankofa:
Look to Your Past Forgotten Heritage

ISBN: 0615610749
ISBN 13: 9780615610740

Library of Congress Control Number: 2012934890
Telos Training Inc.
Westerville, OH

The Power of a
Virtuous Woman

PAULA PENN-NABRIT

Dedication

This book is dedicated to my mother, Sister Mildred Penn, who continues to teach me daily just how much power a virtuous woman has; my late mother-in-law, Mrs. Vernice Nabrit who confirmed that teaching relentlessly for the 35 years I knew her; and my husband, C. Madison, who continues to inspire me to strive to be a powerful woman of virtue-even when I fall far short of the mark. Thank you, Peace & Blessings!

Acknowledgements

I want to thank my pastor, Dr. Eugene Lundy, my assistant pastor, Dr. Glenn Walter, and my assistant Sunday School Superintendent, Sis. Linda Wright, for suggesting I teach an adult woman's Sunday School class. Thank you for continuing your "gentle suggestions" despite my repeated refusals. I have to thank my parents, Bro. and Sis. Penn, who as daily Bible scholars and in various roles as Sunday School teachers, superintendents and church trustee, have shown me the importance of being "not just a hearer but a doer of the Word." Thanks to my big brother David for his smiles of encouragement through the process of writing this book–and especially for reviewing my comments on physics in Chapter 5! And thank you to my sisters, Cheryl, Courtney and Sonjia for helping me flesh out this book at its various stages of development over the past five years. Of course I have to thank CMadison-profusely for his willingness to listen to me read (and re-read) these chapters aloud over and over and over. Thanks C for the editorial comments and the good, constructive, grammatical feedback–even when I didn't want to hear it! But most of all I have to thank the 20+ sisters in our women's Sunday School class; without you I would not have written The Power of a Virtuous Woman. And I have to give a special thank you to Karmeil Stepter for arriving early *every* Sunday to set up our class room, start the coffee and tea and just going out of her way to create a space for excellence. And to my dear daughter-in-law, Tanika Nabrit, for making sure the clean-up happened every week. Thank you. Finally, a great big and truly heartfelt thanks to each and every sister who has ever been a part of our class, from the first 9 who met back in 2007 to the 25 of us "regulars" who meet together now. Thank you for your prayers, your participation, your probative questions and most of all for the genuine sisterhood we have created, developed and nurtured together. It is a rare and beautiful thing and I am blessed to be a part of it.

Table of Contents

Introduction

I began writing this book in 2007 for our Sunday School class. The original objective was to explore holistically the purpose, function and true nature of women and of virtue – all through the lens of Proverbs 31.

One chapter of one book of the Bible doesn't seem like enough to warrant weeks of study and discussion. Especially considering the fact many of us have been "in church" most, if not all of our lives. We know this chapter and have heard it, and the supporting scriptures discussed numerous times. And I am certainly NOT holding myself out as some perfected example of a virtuous woman. But I think we, as a community of sisters, can, help each other "dig a little deeper" in God's word, especially as it relates to us.

We know a lot already, at least on some level; and much of what we know we learned from our mothers and grandmothers and great-grandmothers. But some of what we have been taught we have discarded. Some we discarded without thinking; some we discarded because of outside influences. It's easy to forget the admonition in 2 Corinthians 6:17 "*Wherefore come out from among them, and be ye separate.*" Some we discarded out of a lack of respect for the work our mothers did and the paths they laid out for us. Regardless of the reason(s), maybe we need to go back and retrieve, at least, some of it.

In Asanti, a Ghanaian language, "Sankofa" loosely interpreted means "look to your past, forgotten heritage". What did our foremothers know about the word of God and how did they use it to do such great things with such limited resources? I'm not advocating a return to long dresses, closed shoes and unprocessed hair-well, I am kind of an advocate of unprocessed hair, but we need to go back and examine our past and the Word of God.

I want a deeper understanding of Holiness as a theology of liberation. I want a deeper understanding of submission as strength. And while I love Aretha Franklin's "Natural Woman", I want more than a feeling brought about by the closeness of a man. I want to explore the process of becoming the natural woman God intended me to become. How can I help (or love) someone else without first knowing who God intended for me to be?

I don't immediately flash to a theme song when the topic of Sunday School comes up, but in thinking about this class, an old song just kept running through my mind. I can't remember the last time I heard anyone actually sing it but the lyrics are perfect for a class about the power of virtuous women.

> *"I've got a river of life flowing out of me,*
> *makes the lame to walk and the blind to see,*
> *Opens prison doors, sets the captives free.*
> *I've got a river life flowing out of me.*
>
> *Spring up O well, within my soul,*
> *Spring up O well, that makes me whole,*
> *Spring up O well, and give to me,*
> *More life, abundantly."*

My Sisters, Thank you for agreeing to take this journey of exploration with me.

CHAPTER 1

"Mean What You Say and Say What You Mean."

Terminology & Definitions: Secular, Spiritual & Colloquial.

English is a precise tool. That fact is far from obvious in today's society where people incorrectly conjugate verbs, refuse to match verb tense to subject, mispronounce words and generally abuse the language, making up words as nouns, verbs, adjectives and adverbs as they go. Granted language is constantly evolving, but there remain rules of grammar, syntax and punctuation that exist to help us communicate. When those rules are broken whether intentionally or out of inattention or ignorance, the process of communication can be compromised. Nowhere is that more apparent than in the area of definition. How can we dictate "Mean what you say and say what you mean" if we all have different definitions of the words we are using? So, as a point of clarification, I want to begin with an examination of the terminology *(term: a word or group of words designating something, terminology: the terms belonging to a specialized subject)* and definition *(define: to state the meaning of a word or a phrase; definition: the act of defining or making definite, distinct, or clear)* of the title of this course. In the weeks to come I will try to be careful to define and clarify all the words that I use. That way, if we disagree, and no doubt we will, at least we will know about what we are disagreeing.

The course title seems simple and self-explanatory, The Power of a Virtuous Woman. But what do these words really mean? How has God defined these terms? What do we mean when we use them? And most importantly, are our meanings compatible with God's meanings? Let's examine our words carefully, because "death and life are in the power of the tongue." Proverbs 18:21.

Grammatically, *The* is a definite as opposed to an indefinite article; it indicates specificity as opposed to generality. Spiritually, we see this distinction when we read John 1:1 *"In the beginning was the Word,…"* It doesn't say "In the beginning was *a* Word." It is written with specificity. All world religions have their own holy scriptures, but we know the Bible is *The* Word of God. Here is a secular example of the specificity of the definite article. I have a husband, a father, an older brother, two brothers-in-law, five adult nephews and three adult sons, but whether they're all over for a cook-out or I am home alone, my husband is *the* man of the house. I love the other men I listed, but they are each but *a* man in relation to me and my household. Finally, we hear the colloquial distinction between the definite and indefinite article all the time when folks refer to someone with authority as *"The* Man!" And in the black community we certainly know there is a world of difference between dealing with "a" white man and "the" white man.

Power is a part of speech known as a noun, a person, place or thing, and is defined as the ability to do or act; strength, might, force. Spiritually, those of us who have received the infilling of the Holy Ghost, evidenced by speaking in other tongues can and should "act" on the promise stated in Acts 1:8 *"But ye shall receive power after that the Holy Ghost is come upon you…"*. But even in the Old Testament there is the promise of boundless, regenerating power actualized by faith seen in Isaiah 40:29. *"He giveth power to the faint; and to them that have no might he increaseth strength."* Colloquially we often hear people say, "Girl he got it like that" and as the receiver of the message we infer the person actually has power to make things happen.

Of is a preposition, a word used as a modifier to indicate derivation, origin, connection, qualities or attributes. Spiritually, we see the critical use of the preposition as indicative of the origin or source of our ideal state of mind in 2 Timothy1:7 *"For God hath not given us the spirit of fear, but of power, and of love, and of a sound mind."* Colloquially we may hear a mother berate her child with "You know you know better–What were you thinking of?!"

A, an indefinite article, i.e., there is more than one. Spiritually, we have to be careful not to think or believe that we are the only one. In 1 Kings 19:14 Elijah makes that prideful mistake, *"and I, even I only, am left…"*. But God shows him in 1 Kings 19:18 *"Yet I have left me seven thousand in Israel, all the knees which have not bowed unto Baal, and every mouth which hath not kissed him."* We can and should strive to be *a* virtuous woman, in the broadest sense of the word, but we should never, ever think of ourselves as *the* virtuous woman, for there are in fact many virtuous women among us in the body of Christ.

Similarly, in the colloquial, when the song says "She's a brick house" we know that means the woman has *a* beautiful body, but not the only beautiful body. That is an important distinction to remember because physical beauty is not only temporal or fleeting, it is also a rather common occurrence. There are many beautiful women.

Virtuous is an adjective defined as conforming to moral and ethical principles; having or showing virtue. *Virtue* is a noun and there are two forms or categories. One category refers to the *natural virtues,* namely any moral virtue of which humankind is capable, especially the *cardinal virtues* justice, temperance, prudence and fortitude. The other category refers to *theological virtues*, i.e., faith, hope and charity; and these, by definition, are infused into the human intellect and will by a special grace of God. These are the secular definitions of virtue and virtuous. We see more detailed definitions in the scriptures. In different translations of Mark 5:30 we see virtue used as a synonym for power. The King James Version reads "*And Jesus, immediately know- ing in himself that virtue had gone out of him, turned him about in the press, and said, Who touched my clothes?*" Yet in <u>The New American Standard Bible</u> and many other translations, the text reads, "*Immediately Jesus, perceiving in Himself that the power proceeding from Him had gone forth, turned around in the crowd and said, 'Who touched My garments?'*". 2 Peter 1: 5-7 also seems to equate virtue with power "*add to your faith virtue; and to virtue knowledge; And to knowledge temperance; and to tem- perance patience; and to patience godliness; And to godliness brotherly kind- ness; and to brotherly kindness charity*." Patience, kindness and charity would have been known to Peter as natural or moral virtues so his earlier admonition seems to equate virtue with power just as we saw in Mark.

Elsewhere, we see proof of virtue as its own reward in Philippians 4:8, "*Finally brethren, whatsoever things are true, whatsoever things are honest, whatsoever things are just, whatsoever things are pure, whatsoever things are lovely, whatsoever things are of good report; if there be any virtue, and if there be any praise, think on these things.*" *Virtue* is not gender-specific and is a valid and noble pursuit for men as well as women. Spiritually, one thing is absolutely certain, virtue encompasses a broader vista than just the sexual purity of women!

Woman is a noun defined as the female human being or an adult female person. This secular definition is primarily biological in its scope. But we exist as more than merely physical or biological beings. How did God design and define woman? Genesis 1:27 illustrates God's design for woman as identical to that of man in that both were created by God and in the image of God. "*So God created man in his own image, in the image of God created he him; male and female created he them.*" God's design included a strategic plan for our time on the planet and our interaction with the other life forms He created. Genesis 1:28 "*And God blessed them, and God said unto them, Be fruitful, and multiply, and replenish the earth, and subdue it: and have dominion over the fish of the sea, and over the fowl of the air, and over every living thing that moveth upon the earth.*" God's process for the design of woman was derivative or taken from man thus ensuring biological compatibility. Genesis 2:22 "*And the rib, which the LORD God had taken from man, made he a woman, and brought her unto the man.*"

So there we have it, a detailed analysis and examination of our course title, The Power of a Virtuous Woman. Now that we have deepened our knowledge/wisdom, let's look at our applications as critical indicators of our understanding. "*Wisdom is the principle thing; therefore get wisdom: and with all thy getting get understanding.*" Proverbs 4:7.

CHAPTER 1 QUESTIONS

1. Are you comfortable thinking of yourself as a powerful person?

    _____

    _____

    _____

2. How does your sense of yourself as a powerful person (or not) affect your relationships with others?

    _____

    _____

    _____

3. What are your greatest strengths?

    _____

    _____

    _____

4. How do your strengths benefit others?

    _____

    _____

    _____

5. Where do you desire to be strengthened?

    _____

    _____

    _____

6. Are you comfortable thinking of yourself as a virtuous woman?

_____

_____

_____

7. Do you think others view you as a virtuous woman?

_____

_____

_____

8. Which virtues do you possess?

_____

_____

_____

9. How do your virtues benefit others?

_____

_____

_____

10. Which virtues do you want to acquire?

CHAPTER 2

_____

_____

_____

"Conjunction, Junction, What's Your Function?"

To understand the function of a thing (or a woman) one must first know and understand its designed purpose, its greatest good, its end, its telos. Aristotle (paraphrased)

W hy was Woman created? What was our designed purpose? Is our current function consistent?

τελος [télos] is a Greek word for the ultimate end, goal or purpose of a thing. In the natural, non-human universe the telos of each thing occurs automatically unless there is an intervening force. For example the telos of an acorn is to become an oak tree. Unless the acorn is eaten by a squirrel or the young tree is washed away by soil erosion or struck by lightening in a storm, it will become an oak tree; its telos will be achieved.

For humans the telos often seems shrouded in mystery. For centuries philosophers have developed whole systems of thought and analysis around the question of humanity's telos and what it means in terms of correct human behavior. Teleological systems are based on the idea that if we know our ultimate goal or end then actions that move us closer are right and those that move us away are wrong. Of course teleological systems still leave us with the problem of defining our individual human telos. The other approach is a deontological system where the focus shifts from our telos to our duty. In this framework, everything that conforms to our duty is right and everything that does not conform to our duty is wrong. But again we are left with the underlying question of what is our duty. And really, that question of the human duty is no less a mystery than the question of the human telos. What is sadly surprising is how often we see this same set of questions broached by saints of God, filled with the Holy Ghost. This should not be so because in the beauty of Holiness we know that teleological and deontological systems are joined through Christ and the simple and perfect plan He has for us and our lives. Of course the fact that something is simple does not mean that it is easy.

Let us examine what God has determined to be our telos and our duty as women. Once we have determined that, we can explore how close we are to conformity. Understanding our God-designed telos and duty will also help us understand better the text of the virtuous woman outlined in Proverbs 31. So, starting at the beginning of the Word of God, in the book of Genesis 1:1-31, we see God's "journal". His daily activities are listed and described. On the first day He created heaven, earth, light, day and night. On the second day He divided the waters and called the separating firmament Heaven. The third day was especially busy, He gathered all the dry land under heaven and called it earth, named the waters Seas and had the earth bring forth grass and herbs and fruit trees-all yielding seed "in itself, after his kind". As an aside it is interesting to note that the idea of "reproducible parts" did not begin with the United States, the cotton gin, the peculiar institution of slavery or the Industrial revolution. On the fourth day God established time, seasons, the sun, moon and stars. He created whales, fish and birds on the fifth day. On the sixth day God made all the animals on the earth and *"man in his own image, in the image of God created he him; male and female created he them"* Genesis 1:27.

The last things God created, on the last day of His creation were male and female images of Himself. But in the second chapter of Genesis we see that God did not create male and female at the same moment of time, even though it was on the same day. *"God formed man of the dust of the ground, and breathed into his nostrils the breath of life; and the man became a living soul."* Genesis 2:7. Here we see the most unique and special quality of humans over all other life forms, including other mammals. Many other mammals are sentient, meaning they have awareness through their senses and they have a form of consciousness. When our sons were small we had three black Labrador retrievers, Shadrach, Meshach and Abednago. The dogs were incredibly intelligent and even knew when it was time for me to pick the boys up from school! But as sentient as they were, the Bible does not say that God blew the breath of life into the nostrils of any mammals other than man, thus providing the miraculous wonder of a living soul.

After creating man as a living soul, God *"planted a garden eastward in Eden"* complete with trees and rivers and gold and onyx and bdellium (an aromatic gum residue similar to myrrh); and it was in this garden that God gave Adam specific instructions about the tree of knowledge of good and evil. Genesis 2:8-17. Notice that the Woman had not been created when these instructions were given to Adam. At the end of all this, still on the sixth day, God decided to make woman. Genesis 2:18 *"And the LORD God said, It is not good that the man should be alone; I will make him an help meet for him."* The King James Version of that verse clarifies *"helpmeet"* as a *"helper comparable to him"*. Essentially, God created man, observed him in the environment created for him and decided that man, good creation that he was, would be better with a companion, so God made woman. *"...and God saw everything that he had made, and behold, it was very good. And the evening and the morning were the sixth day."* Genesis 1:31.

We now see the purpose of woman, the telos of our creation is to be a helpmeet for man. The teleological rationale for our actions can be viewed through the lens of that purpose or highest good. The deontological rationale is equally clear; the duty of a woman, our duty, is to be a helpmeet. Adam, when presented with God's creation of a helpmeet, called her *"Woman, because she was taken out of Man."* Genesis 2:23. The Hebrew word is Ishshah. <u>Strong's Hebrew Bible Dictionary</u> defines Ishshah as follows: "feminine of 'iysh' or 'enowsh'; a woman, each, every female, wife, woman." Interestingly, <u>Strong's</u> also defines the word as: "the same as 'eshshah', but used in a liturgical sense; properly a burnt-offering; but occasionally of any *sacrifice* (emphasis mine) made by fire." So there is an element of sacrifice in the very word for woman. Adam sacrificed a rib for her creation, and woman must sacrifice some part of herself to operate effectively as a helpmeet. Again, we see the simplicity of the union of the telos and the duty, but also we see that it is not easy. Knowing that challenge, how surprised can we be at the first Woman's initial failure to use her power for good. Genesis 3:6 states *"And when the woman saw that the tree was good for food, and that it was pleasant to the eyes, and a tree to be desired to make one wise, she took of the fruit thereof, and did eat, and gave also unto her husband with her; and he did eat."*

The woman was beguiled by the serpent; that was her weakness. Her failure was her inability to understand and her unwillingness to act on her duty to fulfill her telos as a helpmeet. Her sin surely was not a help to Adam! But this is not just the first example of sin, often preached (harped on) by men. This is also the first biblical example of Woman's power to influence the behavior of man. 1 Timothy 2:14 *"And it was not Adam who was deceived, but the woman being deceived, fell into transgression."* We see Adam was not deceived or beguiled by the serpent. He was influenced so much so by the Woman that he disobeyed the direct order given to him – not to them – by God directly. As women, we must never forget the enormous power of influence we have over the men in our lives. And we must pray daily that God will give us the wisdom to use our power for good.

But what of the consequences to Woman for allowing herself to be beguiled? And what exactly does it mean to be beguiled? To beguile is to influence, mislead and delude by trickery, flattery or charm. Synonyms for beguile include entranced, captivated, delighted, enthralled and enchanted, "influenced by charms and incantations". It almost sounds hypnotic and as every woman knows, that kind of attention can be dangerous and has been the basis of many seductions. Have you ever felt "under the spell" of a man? Did it happen by his constantly ignoring you or by his constant attention? Usually attention is at the heart of beguilement and seduction. Could the Woman have been beguiled if Adam's attentions had been focused on her? Often we hear discussion of the question of Adam's physical location, but even when physically present, one's mind and attention may be elsewhere. But regardless of Adam's attention – or lack thereof – the Woman allowed herself to be beguiled, and as a consequence, punishment is meted out. The nature of her punishment, and by extension our punishment, is multi-dimensional and somewhat complex.

Genesis 3:16 *"Unto the woman he said, I will greatly multiply thy sorrow and thy conception; in sorrow thou shalt bring forth children; and thy desire shall be to thy husband, and he shall rule over thee."* There is a lot in this verse, enough to warrant a *"line upon line, precept upon precept"* examination and analysis. I have broken the punishment that some have called a curse into five elements:

  (i)   *"I will greatly multiply thy sorrow"*
 (ii)   *"and thy conception;"*
(iii)   *"in sorrow thou shalt bring forth children;"*
 (iv)   *"and thy desire shall be to thy husband,"*
  (v)   *"and he shall rule over thee."*

(i) God's opening statement, *"I will greatly multiply thy sorrow,"* implies sorrow already was present —even in the Garden. Might the Woman's sorrow have been the absence of attention from Adam? The scripture is not clear on this point. What is clear is that whatever sorrow the Woman had was to be multiplied as a result of her sin. This is a sad, but all too common, occurrence. We feel ignored; we decide to take care of it ourselves; we step outside of our telos and our duty; and when it is over, when we are finished with having our way instead of God's way, our sorrow is multiplied. James 1:14 articulates this point with frightening clarity: *"But every man is tempted, when he is drawn away of his own lust, and enticed. Then when lust hath conceived, it bringeth forth sin: and sin, when it is finished, bringeth forth death."* God showed grace and mercy by supplanting multiplied sorrow for death, but that was not the end of the punishment.

(ii) God multiplied the Woman's sorrow *"and thy conception"*. What exactly does that mean? We know that God already said to be fruitful and multiply and replenish the earth, but the process was not initially clarified. Maybe conception and pregnancy as we now know it were not in the original plan. Maybe there was no "morning sickness" or varicose veins or stretch marks or insane cravings. Maybe conception and pregnancy originally were designed to be as pleasant and painless as the Woman's derivation from Man. Regardless of what we might speculate here, the fact remains God multiplied our sorrow and our conception.

God also dictated that sorrow would be the context of childbirth,(iii) *"in sorrow thou shalt bring forth children"* but again He displays grace and mercy. It is the amazing grace and mercy of God that the fear and pain of labor and delivery do not leave permanent and traumatic emotional scars. Like many of you, my husband and I often look back and laugh about the details of each of our children's births. As women we continue to reap what the first Woman sowed, but how gracious of God to allow us to reap in mercy and to ultimately enjoy the fruits of our conception!

(iv) This next piece of Woman's judgment is challenging because it (almost) seems unfair; *"...thy desire shall be to thy husband..."* Why did God not dictate mutual desire? Did God know or assume that the husband would always desire his wife? It just doesn't seem balanced does it? But the fact is, as told in Isaiah 55: 8 and 9, God's plans do not have to be fair or even make sense to us. *"For my thoughts are not your thoughts, neither are your ways my ways, saith the Lord. For as the heavens are higher than the earth, so are my ways higher than your ways, and my thoughts than your thoughts."* And here is the wonderful promise about obedience, Isaiah 55: 10-13 *"For as the rain cometh down, and the snow from heaven, and returneth not thither, but watereth the earth, and maketh it bring forth and bud, that it may give seed to the sower, and bread to the eater: So shall my word be that goeth forth out of my mouth: it shall not return unto me void, but it shall accomplish that which I please, and it shall prosper in the thing whereto I sent it. For ye shall go out with joy, and be led forth with peace: the mountains and the hills shall break forth before you into singing, and all the trees of the field shall clap their hands. Instead of the thorn shall come up the fir tree, and instead of the brier shall come up the myrtle tree: and it shall be to the LORD for a name, for an everlasting sign that shall not be cut off."* How cool is that, to be able to go out with joy and be led forth with peace and to have mountains and hills and trees singing and clapping their hands? It makes obedience seem worth it.

(v) And if the imbalance of desire is a hard pill to swallow, look at this *"and he shall rule over thee."* We see it reiterated in the New Testament, so we cannot escape it even through this dispensation of grace. 1 Corinthians 11:3 clearly restates the edict of Genesis *"But I would have you know, that the head of every man is Christ; and the head of the woman is the man; and the head of Christ is God"*. Granted the concept of headship must be recognized by all within the body of Christ, but Woman alone is singled out for the complete and total headship held by another mere mortal, warts, farts and all.

So now we have explored in a way that we may not have explored it before, the expansive parameters of our existence, our telos and our duty as Woman created by God. I find it interesting that often we are far more willing to accept the terms and conditions of conception and pregnancy, labor and delivery than those of the submission of our desire and our will to our husbands. That may be due to the fact that we have no collective memory of submission to man. Genesis 1:27 simply says *"in the image of God created He him; male and female created He them"*. Later in Genesis 1:27 *"It is not good that the man should be alone; I will make him an helpmeet for him"*. No where in God's journal entries of creation does He state that man is to have dominion or rule over Woman. Woman's submission to Man is the direct consequence of Woman's sin; it does not appear to be part of God's original plan of creation. That may be why it is so hard for so many of us to conform to the perfect will of God in our relationships with our husbands. Yet, to struggle against the articulated will of God is foolish, no matter how rational our reasons.

The obligation of submission is not a contingent one. Marriage is a contract, a covenant relationship between God, the party of the first part; the husband, the party of the second part and the wife, the party of the third part. Legally, some contractual conditions are deemed "contingent". Simply stated my performance is contingent or conditioned on the performance of the other party to the contract. If I work for you, and you stop paying me, I can stop working. Conversely, if I stop working you can stop paying me. Our obligations to each other are contingent. However, not all contractual obligations are contingent; some are non-contingent, meaning my performance obligations are not tied to the successful or satisfactory performance of the other party to the contract. Our spiritual obligations are non-contingent. More specifically, our marital obligations are non-contingent. The scripture creates no conditional performance allowance. The husband is the head of the wife because those are the terms stipulated by God. A husband's periodic (or even constant) inadequate performance as the head does not eliminate the contractual obligation to be submissive.

This concept of a non-conditional contract does not conform to rational thought and is inconsistent with secular philosophies; but again, *"His ways are not our ways"*. That's why we should not encourage one another when we hear things like "Girl, I can do bad by myself!" Nor should we offer up unhealthy and unsolicited commentary like "Girl, shoot, I wouldn't a bit more take that – ain't you got a job?!" It is not that those statements are irrational; sometimes they are very rational. Sadly, some men are far, far, far away from what the Lord has called them to be, but again, our obligation of submission is not contingent on any man's performance.

As Paul discovered, the rational mind, in and of itself is not sufficient. We need a revelation from God and the necessary faith to receive it and walk in it. In Acts 9:5 Paul asks a critical question and receives not only an answer but a proverb to go with it. *"And he said, Who art thou, Lord? And the Lord said, I am Jesus whom thou persecutest: it is hard for thee to kick against the pricks."* It is hard to kick against the pricks is a Syriac (Aramaic) proverb. Pricks are goads, or traditional farming implements used to guide oxen. They are similar to cattle prods and when stubborn oxen kick back against the goads or pricks, they injure themselves. When we "kick back" against God's plan, we too injure ourselves. This is true even when we try to hide our stubbornness in what I like to call "church talk" or extra sacrifices.

Church talk and sacrifice is often what we use to camouflage our rebellious spirit. When I do not want to submit to my husband, I do not say "I'm more than 3 times 7 and I work every day-you can't tell me what to do!" No, instead I use church talk and say "I have to be about my Father's work in the temple". I tell my girlfriends "It's a sacrifice to face my husband's anger about a lack of well-balanced meals and a clean house, but I am like Mary, I have taken 'the better part'." But in Luke 10:38-42, the story of the sisters Mary and Martha, there is no mention of husbands or children. Our refusal to be in submission to our husbands is disobedience, regardless of whether our husbands "deserve" our obedience. Our obedience is ultimately to God and He will not be satisfied or pacified with anything less, nor will He be fooled by our well-crafted justifications. This is brilliantly illuminated in 1 Samuel 15:22-23 when Samuel chastises Saul and informs him that the kingdom has been taken from him.

God told Saul to destroy the city of Amalek, kill all the Amalekites and destroy everything and everyone with them. Saul decided to spare the Kenites because they had spared the children of Israel earlier. He also decided to spare the Amalekite king Agog along with the best of the sheep and oxen. These were not unreasonable or irrational decisions; but, and here's the critical part, they were not Saul's decisions to make! God had already decided. In fact, He is "The Decider," not President Bush, and mercy was not what God had decided in this instance. To make matters worse, when confronted with his disobedience, Saul tried to rationalize it with the dreaded "church talk". He told Samuel that he was going to use the spoil which should have been destroyed as a sacrifice to God. Samuel's words to Saul should echo in our ears. *"And Samuel said, Hath the LORD as great delight in burnt offerings and sacrifices, as in obeying the voice of the LORD? Behold, to obey is better than sacrifice, and to hearken than the fat of rams. For rebellion is as the sin of witchcraft, and stubbornness is as iniquity and idolatry."* The same message is conveyed in Mark 12:33 *"And to love Him with all the heart and with all the understanding and with all the strength...is much more than all burnt offerings and sacrifices."* John 14:15 says it even more simply, *"If you love me, keep my commandments"*.

We are each unique and special creations of God, but we have to be cautious less we become so enthralled with our individuality, our gifts and fruits and callings that we forget the axiom in 1 Corinthians 14:40 *"Let all things be done decently and in order"*; and verse 33 *"For God is not the author of confusion (disorder), but of peace..."*. Every individual gift and calling that is of God can and will work, according to, not against His plan. Let me interject an "I" statement here.

I do not believe He is going to call me, into some immediate ministry the work of which would be in contradiction to the plan already laid out for me as a woman, a wife and a mother. It took God a minute or two to season and prepare Moses for the call on his life. His years with Pharaoh's daughter and his years with Reuel in Midian were long ones, but nowhere does the scripture say that Moses was bored or resentful of the tasks placed before him. Moses knew the wisdom in the Word of God, Ecclesiastes 3:1, *"To every thing there is a season, and a time to every purpose under the heaven"*. As an educated woman in the 21st century it is easy to think I am exempted from the telos and duty outlined by God in the beginning of His creation. And regrettably, even in the church, I can find much support for that disobedience couched in the church talk of "God's doing a new thing!" But does God's new thing ever contradict His old things? 2 Corinthians 10:4-5 is not just a word of caution about the secular world, it is a word of caution about our own thoughts and desires that are not in right relationship with the Word of God. *"For the weapons of our warfare are not carnal, but mighty through God to the pulling down of strong holds; Casting down imaginations, and every high thing that exalteth itself against the knowledge of God, and bringing into captivity every thought to the obedience of Christ."*

Let us try to support one another in the endless effort to bring every one of our thoughts into captivity to the obedience of Christ. That is the only way that we can know, understand and implement the telos and duty of our lives as women of God. Obedience is better than sacrifice and I don't know about you, but I want to *"go out with joy, and be led forth with peace"*.

CHAPTER 2 QUESTIONS

1. Telos, duty, helpmeet. Does any of that make sense today?

    _____

    _____

    _____

2. Is God's judgment on Woman still operating as a punishment or a curse?

    _____

    _____

    _____

3. How might I view God's judgment of Woman as a blessing?

    _____

    _____

    _____

4. Which is greater, the power to control or the power to influence?

    _____

    _____

    _____

5. Which type of power did Woman use in the Garden of Eden?

    _____

    _____

    _____

6. Do you think the Woman knew or understood the power she had before she ate the fruit?

_____

_____

_____

7. Can you exercise power and be in submission at the same time?

_____

_____

_____

8. Do you think today's women have untapped power?

_____

_____

_____

9. If so, where do you think that power lies?

_____

_____

_____

10. Are we more aware of our potential power in our churches and communities than in our homes?

_____

_____

_____

11. Are we using our power for good works in the church or the community as an excuse to not be a helpmeet?

_____

_____

_____

12. Do you think the power potential of women is why men resort to sexism, domination and oppression of women?

_____

_____

_____

13. As there are no accidents in God, what do you think He wants us to do with the power He has given us?

_____

_____

_____

14. On a personal level, do you think God is pleased with your use of power in your home?

_____

_____

_____

15. List three things you can start doing in your home this week to better exercise the power God gave you.

_____

_____

_____

CHAPTER 3

"Who Is She and What Is She to You?"

Whose advice can or will we accept? Who has
"earned the right" to provide it?

Who is Lemuel's mother? What do we know about
Bathsheba? Do you think she felt "reduced" by being
referred to by relationship, i.e., as someone's mother,
rather than by her individual identity? Who is Lemuel? What do we
know about Solomon? At the time of this conversation he's an adult.
Why is he still willing to listen to his mother?

Typically, a discussion of the famous scripture on the virtuous woman begins at verse 10 and moves rather quickly to all the work this

seemingly inexhaustible and bionic woman accomplishes. The orga-
nizational wizardry and efficient multi-tasking of this sister are worth
noting-and we will examine her skills in detail later. But for now,
let's begin with a careful reading of this pivotal chapter from the
beginning.

Proverbs 31: "*The words of king Lemuel, the prophecy that his mother taught
him.*"

The King James Version states that this king is presented with a
"prophecy" by his mother. Parallel translations use other words such
as teaching, declaration, oracle, burden and prophetic revelation, but
the intent is clear. A word of correction has come forth. Who is this
woman who is able to give a prophetic word and a word of correction no less to a man who has already come into a position of power
and authority? How was she able to capture and hold the attention
of her son? At the time of this event Lemuel is well past the age of
her control. It is far too late in the game for "time outs", spankings
or any other form of punishment or physical discipline. What must
have already transpired in this woman's relationship with her child
that enabled her to approach him courageously with "a word" when
she felt he needed it?

This encounter is especially striking when we think about when
this conversation occurred. Single parent, female-headed households
were rare and generally the result of widowhood rather than choice.
There were no socially accepted "alternative" lifestyles in Israel. There
had been no women's movement within the experience of the children of Israel, not in Egypt, not in the wilderness, not under Saul's
rule or David's reign. Women could not speak in the temple nor hold
the position of the priest. Yet despite the dominant political view of
women as "less than", this woman did what many people now, both
male and female, are afraid to do; she "spoke truth to power". And
forget power for a minute, many mothers and fathers today long to

be able to speak (peaceably!) a word of wisdom to their school age and adolescent children, much less those that are already adults. Even if Solomon did not heed all the admonitions of his mother, and we know that he did not; at least he listened!

We need to know Bathsheba's secret. How did she get her son to listen? Because if we cannot get our own spawn (the issue of a parent or family. See <u>American Heritage Dictionary</u>) to listen to us; how, literally, in the name of God, can we speak a word to any other children in our community who so desperately need it? As black women, wives, mothers, grandmothers, sisters and aunties, we know that the idea of "other people's children" is a luxury we can ill afford. We cannot stand by, shake our heads and suck our teeth as yet another generation of our young emerge like wild, feral dogs loose on the land. And yes I know "that's not all of 'em" but the fact is one is too many. We cannot afford to lose one more of our communal sons or daughters. Isn't that at least one interpretation of the parable of the lost sheep presented in Matthew 18:12? *"How think ye? if a man have an hundred sheep, and one of them be gone astray, doth he not leave the ninety and nine, and goeth into the mountains, and seeketh that which is gone astray?"* When the Shepard realizes one sheep is lost, does the shepherd say, well "that's not all of 'em"?! No, the good shepherd goes out and looks for the one that has gone astray. Surely sheep are not more valuable than our children-even if they're grown (or think they are!)

But before we get ahead of ourselves, let us look at what we know about Lemuel. There is some speculation about Lemuel because the scriptures do not definitely identify him. Some Bible scholars identify him as an imaginary character, some think this is a reference to Hezekiah, others think this may be a reference to a Lemuel who was king of Massa, or some other Arabian prince. But a great many scholars believe this is a reference to Solomon. And for the purposes of this book, that is how I choose to deal with this text. We will proceed under the theory that Lemuel is Solomon. And once we decide that Lemuel is Solomon then we know that the mother in question is none other than Bathsheba. Given what people say about Bathsheba and the speculation, even today, that it was her fault David saw her bathing, her fault he lusted after her, her fault David had her husband killed, given all that "fault," isn't it wonderful to see her depicted at the end of her life as the virtuous woman? As an aside, it is quite remarkable how much "power" is attributed to women when it comes to fault or inducement of sin. But I digress; Bathsheba, as the mother of Solomon, was one of the ancestors of Jesus so by way of adoption she stands as one of our spiritual ancestors. She also stands as an example of the kind of perseverance essential for the grace and mercy of God to be brilliantly manifested in the lives of His children. Regardless of what happens to us (or what we let happen) and regardless of the role we play in those events, regardless of the consent or condemnation of others, if we can persevere, all of God's plans for us will emerge, "in the fullness of time." Galatians 4:4 *"But when the fulness of the time was come, God sent forth his Son, made of a woman, made under the law...,"* As women we have an edge in understanding the concept of the fullness of time because our bodies operate in a cyclical process that mirrors the cycles of the moon and tides and seasons created by God.

Thank God that Bathsheba did not have to rely on other humans to decide she was a virtuous woman or was worthy to be called one. Because she knew she was a virtuous woman, she did not have to concern herself with whether or not others recognized it. Perhaps she took a page from David's "playbook" and encouraged herself. *"And David was greatly distressed; for the people spake of stoning him, because the soul of all the people was grieved, every man for his sons and for his daughters: but David encouraged himself in the LORD his God."* 1 Samuel 30:6. Do you think Bathsheba might have been a bit distressed over her situation? Do you think the people may have spoken of stoning her? Do you think the soul of some of the people around her might have been "grieved"? Bathsheba must have been seeking the Lord for real! She knew she was the object of speculation, condemnation, jealousy and envy. She knew every smile was not sincere and was wise enough to know that every shut eye ain't sleep. Bathsheba was young, but she was neither stupid nor inexperienced in the ways of power.

Bathsheba was not just the widow of the warrior Uriah, and a woman shamefully impregnated by David, she was also the granddaughter of Ahithophel, David's trusted counselor. Bathsheba was a woman existing in the world at a time when to be female was to exist at the mercy of and under the protection and almost complete control and domination of male family members. Bathsheba came from a family of power and influence, fully engaged in the drama and intrigue of the kingdom "insiders".

While the prophet Nathan was bold enough to speak directly to David about his sin, it's doubtful that everyone else in the kingdom was that outspoken. Yet, we know that the illicit affair between David and Bathsheba was known, because later in the scriptures we see that Bathsheba's grandfather, Ahithophel, plotted against David, possibly as revenge for this shame on his family. After many years as David's chief counselor before and after David's affair with Bathsheba, Ahithophel waited until David's son Absalom was ready to rebel and then Ahithophel sought his revenge and offered counsel to Absalom against David as detailed in 2 Samuel 16:20-23. Of course, it did not work, because God already had decided to bless David and deliver him out of the hands of his enemies-even his own sons. *"And one told David, saying, Ahithophel is among the conspirators with Absalom. And David said, O Jehovah, I pray thee, turn the counsel of Ahithophel into foolishness."* 2 Samuel 15:31. Ultimately, Ahithophel hanged himself when Absalom refused to follow all his advice; but Ahithophel's revenge had been accomplished.

Absalom, David's beloved son, had sex with David's concubines, publicly on the roof of David's palace. *"And Ahithophel said unto Absalom, Go in unto thy father's concubines, which he hath left to keep the house; and all Israel shall hear that thou art abhorred of thy father: then shall the hands of all that are with thee be strong. So they spread Absalom a tent upon the top of the house; and Absalom went in unto his father's concubines in the sight of all Israel."* 2 Samuel 16:21-22. This public act of disrespect was foretold by the prophet Nathan and was part of David's punishment described in 2 Samuel 12:10-12 *"Now therefore the sword shall never depart from thine house; …, I will raise up evil against thee out of thine own house, and I will take thy wives before thine eyes, and give them unto thy neighbor, and he shall lie with thy wives in the sight of this sun…For thou didst it secretly: but I will do this thing before all Israel, and before the sun."* Prophecy notwithstanding, it would appear that David did not have the relationship with his son Absalom (or any of the others) that Bathsheba had cultivated with their son Solomon.

So we know that Bathesheba was both blessed and burdened through her beauty as well as her family connections. Keep in mind that in that day and time, to be a woman without the protection of powerful men was to exist in a perpetual state of potential victimhood. We see a sadly similar situation today with the reduction in the number of stable, two-parent households. The rate of marriage in the black community has declined precipitously in the last 40 years. When Dr. King delivered his famous "I Have A Dream" speech in 1963, roughly 70% of black households were headed by a married couple. As of 2002 that percentage was 48% according to the Joint Center for Political and Economic Studies. The U.S. Department of Health and Human Services reports that from 1950 to 1997, the proportion of black babies born to unmarried women rose from 18% to 69%. And the Census Bureau's Current Population Survey for 1998 shows black women at 29%, have the lowest rate of marriage with 49% of Hispanic women married and 55% of white women married. The declining number of families existing within the spiritual sanctity and security of marriage is having disastrous results. There have been many studies on the adverse impact on boys raised with an absent father. What is less studied and discussed is the adverse impact on girls and the increased risk of sexual assault within the community at large. Black women face great risk of sexual assault because of the intersection of racism and sexism-plus for hundreds of years, the rape of a black woman was not a crime in this country. Today, as in biblical times, women without the protection of familial male relationships face greater than average risks of assault and abuse. It is also sadly true that, just as in Bathsheba's time, the risk of incest, violent and hidden, is still very much a danger.

Had Bathsheba not been from such a prominent family, she might well have been killed or simply left to live the rest of her life in desolation. This was the fate even David's daughter, Tamar, suffered as a result of the incestuous rape she endured at the hands of her half-brother, Amnon. 2 Samuel 13:14 *"Howbeit he would not hearken unto her voice: but, being stronger than she, forced her, and lay with her."* and 2 Samuel 13:20 *"And Absalom her brother said unto her, Hath Amnon thy brother been with thee? but hold now thy peace, my sister: he is thy brother; regard not this thing. So Tamar remained desolate in her brother Absalom's house."*

Apparently, David and his sons had difficulty with sexual discipline. Further familial challenges included the failure of forgiveness and the thirst for revenge. We know Absalom never forgave his brother Amnon and plotted to murder him years after the fact as put forth at 2 Samuel 13:32. *"... Let not my lord suppose that they have slain all the young men the king's sons; for Amnon only is dead: for by the appointment of Absalom this hath been determined from the day that he forced his sister Tamar."*

Bathsheba knows the reputation of wrath and revenge within David's family as well as her own. We know from the scriptures that Bathsheba's grandfather never forgave David. We can just imagine how the rest of her family reacted towards her. And what of Uriah's family, what must they have thought of Bathsheba? Uriah was not just some foot soldier in David's army. Uriah, the Hittite, was a captain and a man of great valor. In fact he was one of David's famous mighty men described in 2 Samuel 23:8, 39. Everywhere she turned, Bathsheba was an object of gossip and wild speculation and when her pregnancy became known-what do you think that was like? The scriptures do not state that Bathsheba had children by Uriah, so presumably this pregnancy was her first. Instead of the joy and excitement that a pregnancy should generate, she had to experience her first conception and pregnancy in shame and condemnation. I wonder if Bathsheba had any support or comfort or advice from the older women within the kingdom? How supportive are we when we see women struggling with unplanned pregnancies?

But back to Bathsheba, we know she suffered the pain of public humiliation and shame, and we know nobody can make the public scrutiny of a woman's reputation as "stank" as other women. Sadly, that can be true in the church today. And please do not think Bathsheba's beauty generated compassion among her sisters. Can't you just hear it, "I guess she wasn't all that after all!" And what about us, today, in the 21st century? Are we as likely to forgive and support a pretty sister as one we view as a "Plain Jane" or are we secretly pleased at her downfall? The Word tells us *"envy is as cruel/cold as the grave."* Proverbs 27:4. Then, as if she has not suffered enough, the child she bears by David becomes gravely ill. Yet, there is still no succor for Bathsheba because Nathan the prophet tells David that the child's impending death is recompense for their sin. *"Howbeit, because by this deed thou hast given great occasion to the enemies of the LORD to blaspheme, the child also that is born unto thee shall surely die."* 2 Samuel 12:14. Of course Nathan's prophecy included much more suffering for David, but I am certain that as a new mother the predicted death of her baby was all Bathsheba could hear.

We can easily imagine Bathsheba's pain for secretly don't we often vacillate wildly between heaping all the blame on ourselves and renouncing any blame at all? Take a moment and imagine the depth of despair David and Bathsheba must have experienced in hearing the clear pronouncement that in fact this child's life was to be retribution. Imagine how Bathsheba probably hoped against hope that David's prayers and fasting on behalf of their child would change God's mind. And when the child died, imagine the pain, the sorrow and the guilt. I have been told that the death of a child is the single most psychologically stressful thing that can happen in life. For a marriage, such a tragedy is a classic "make or break" situation. Maybe enduring this shared pain brought David and Bathsheba closer. The scriptures do not tell us how Bathsheba processed all of this. All we can do is observe and speculate.

Bathsheba endured all this, the unwanted attention, the unsolicited seduction, the shameful conception and the pregnancy. She endured the relentless gossip behind her back and the ugly, signifying comments in her face. She endured the murder of her 1st husband, Uriah and the "quickie" 2nd marriage to David. Nowhere does the scripture say how Bathsheba felt about any of this. For all we know she loved Uriah and resented David for involving her in this mess. At the very least we know she respected Uriah and she wasn't happy at his death. *"And when the wife of Uriah heard that Uriah her husband was dead, she mourned for her husband."* 2 Samuel 11:26. This is in sharp contrast to Abigail who also had a husband before she married David. But when Nabal died, the scriptures do not say Abigail mourned. 1 Samuel 25:38-42 describes Abigail's response. I especially like this part *"And Abigail hasted, and arose and rode upon an ass, with five damsels of hers that went after her; and she went after the messengers of David, and became his wife."*

On the other hand, maybe Bathsheba resented Uriah for placing his work commitments before her-that attention issue again. We know

Uriah had the opportunity, contrived though it was, to spend the night with his wife once David called him back to Jerusalem. His refusal is portrayed correctly as an indication of his loyalty and commitment. 2 Samuel 11:11. However, as the man's wife, how might you feel if your husband chose to sleep somewhere other than with you because of his sense of duty? Bathsheba might have been flattered or even enjoyed David's attentions, even while being fearful of the potential consequences. We just don't know. What we do know is she engaged in the custom of rooftop bathing, 2 Samuel 11:2. "*And it came to pass in an eveningtide, that David arose from off his bed, and walked upon the roof of the king's house: and from the roof he saw a woman washing herself; and the woman was very beautiful to look upon.*" So we know Bathsheba was washing more than just her face. And we know that because David was "out of order" he saw her in her ritual bathing–and he decided, he planned to take her. This was no "accident". 2 Samuel 11:4, "…*But David tarried still at Jerusalem.*"

Bathsheba was in obedience to the law set forth in Leviticus 15:19–24 regarding ritual cleansing and the "rules of engagement" during menstruation. I am presuming that the bath David witnessed was part of that cleansing ritual after menstruation otherwise how could they both have known with such certainty that Bathsheba's child was his and not Uriah's. If Bathsheba was just taking a bath then she would have been in a similar position to some young women today. You know the ones on Maury. But Bathsheba had only been with one man since her last cycle so she knew beyond the shadow of a doubt whose seed she carried.

We know David saw her naked and lusted after her, which was his first sin in this relationship as described in Matthew 5:27, "…*whosoever looketh on a woman to lust after her hath committed adultery with her already in his heart.*" Through this we have learned the reality of the lust of the eye and the fact that unlike women, who are most often sexually aroused by imagination and touch, men are often aroused by imagination and sight. Are we helping the brothers when we allow them to see that which they cannot have?! This modern day insight into aspects of human sexual arousal adds another dimension to the New Testament exhortations to modesty put forward in 1 Timothy 2:9-10. *"In like manner also, that women adorn themselves in modest apparel, with shamefacedness and sobriety; not with broided hair, or gold, or pearls, or costly array;..."*

Here is what else we know: Bathsheba endured all of this "baby daddy drama" and the birth of her first child. She endured the worry over the baby's illness and the incredible pain and guilt from the baby's death. She endured all this and did not collapse under the weight of it. Bathsheba sounds like a Sister to me! While she undoubtedly knew David began his downward spiral with her by not being where he was supposed to be, 2 Samuel 11:1, she let it go. She moved forward, had her second child, Solomon, and ultimately became David's favorite wife. That is how we know she let it go. If Bathsheba had continued to hound David about his past, his lust, deceit, murder and the subsequent death of their baby, she would NOT have become his favorite wife. She forgave David and he loved her for it. This was not a foregone conclusion because as you well know, most seductions do not have such happy endings. Plus Bathsheba entered David's household not as his first wife, but as his eighth wife. Many generations in advance, Bathsheba essentially epitomized the famous statement uttered by Julius Cesar a mere 47 years before the birth of Jesus Christ, "Veni, Vidi, Vici" which is translated, "I came, I saw, I conquered." Bathsheba was not David's first wife and Solomon was neither David's first or eldest surviving son at the time of his elevation, yet Solomon was the son to whom David transferred his power and his kingdom.

So back to the beginning. By the time Bathsheba is giving her son a word of correction, he is grown. You know he's heard many, many things about "his Moms" over the years. But guess what? Bathsheba, regardless of what folks wanted to "remember" about her, handled her business as David's wife and Solomon's mother. And she handled her business beautifully. That is the reason her son, a grown man of wisdom, wealth and authority was willing to listen to her when she came to him with a word of correction. That is the reason Solomon wasn't worried about anyone calling him a "Mama's boy." Proverbs 19:20 states *"A wise man receives sound council"* and we know Solomon was wise.

CHAPTER 3 QUESTIONS

1. Are you able to accept advice from others?

    _____

    _____

    _____

2. What do you think others have learned from you about listening and being able to accept advice and wise counsel?

    _____

    _____

    _____

3. Are you comfortable offering advice to others?

    _____

    _____

    _____

4. How do you think your past mistakes might help others on their journey?

    _____

    _____

    _____

5. Do you think others are aware of your past mistakes?

    _____

    _____

    _____

6.   Do you think anyone, regardless of her past, can evolve into a virtuous woman?

_____

_____

_____

7.   Do you think your adult children, grandchildren, nieces or nephews would listen if you came to them with a word of correction? Why or why not?

_____

_____

_____

8.   How do you reconcile Bathsheba's decision to correct her son with the common statement today, "God told me to take my hands off him (or her)?"

_____

_____

_____

9.   Do you think your children or grandchildren, nieces or nephews will ever become too old to receive a word of correction?

_____

_____

_____

10. Do you think you are too old for a word of correction? Do you know of anyone you think is worthy to give it to you?

CHAPTER 4

_____

_____

_____

"It's My Life!"

Einstein articulated the law of relativity and the idea that energy is never destroyed, just re-configured. What does that mean for us and our place in the nuclear, extended and universal family? How does this relate to issues of ancestry, lineage, learned behavior and cultural norms? But I'm getting off track-again. We can come back to those questions later, for now let's examine the next scripture verse.

Proverbs 31:2 *"What, my son? and what, the son of my womb? and what, the son of my vows?"*

Why does Bathsheba call Solomon her son in three different ways? What is Bathsheba showing Solomon about his alleged individuality and where he fits in the big food chain? These are some of the questions begging to be explored in this verse.

Bathsheba is a woman, in every sense of the word. By that I mean more than her biological status as a female human. Bathsheba is a mature, wise, "sure 'nuf grown" woman–and she knows it. Bathsheba is not a woman because she has had her menses. She is not a woman because she has had sexual intercourse. She is not a woman because she has been married. She is not a woman because she has had a child. Bathsheba is not a woman because she has been loved by a man and certainly not because a man has lusted after her. Bathsheba's status as a woman is established by her actions. She has handled herself, her humiliation, her heartaches and her husband–remember she did become David's favorite wife. This is an interesting point as Bathsheba was David's eighth wife. And of David's many concubines and wives only one is recorded in the scriptures to have actually loved David. In 1 Samuel 18:20 and again in verse 28 we are told that Michal, David's first wife, loved him. *"And Michal Saul's daughter loved David: and they told Saul, and the thing pleased him." "And Saul saw and knew that the LORD was with David, and that Michal Saul's daughter loved him."* Perhaps Bathsheba, undoubtedly knowing of David's seeming lack of reciprocity or even regard for Michal's love, wisely decided that love, or in this case probably passion was not enough. I don't think Bathsheba was foreshadowing Tina Turner's question "What's Love Got To Do With It?," but the fact that Bathsheba brought something with more depth than just love to her party is brilliantly illuminated in the scriptures. And because of that depth she was able to handle her husband David. Given that, I doubt she had any concern or question about her ability to handle their son.

Please note that the definition of handle is not limited to manipulative control or domination. Bathsheba presents us with a much broader and panoramic view of the word than its current, customary usage. Dictionary.com Unabridged gives many definitions of handle including "to manage, deal with or be responsible for" as in "I really admire how she handles everything so responsibly". The word "handle" is derivative, it comes from "hand" whose multiple definitions include "means, agency, assistance, aid, instrumentality or cooperation" as in "Please give me a hand with this table". Based on these secular or worldly definitions, we see that in fact Bathsheba did "handle" her business. Also, please note how smoothly the secular or worldly definitions of "handle" and "hand" merge with the Godly telos or purpose of Woman as a helpmeet. And colloquially, in the realm of cultural politics, we see that same merger mirrored in the lyrics "Let's give the boy a hand" from Deniece Williams' long ago hit, "Let's Hear It For the Boy". But back to Bathsheba.

Let's watch how Bathsheba handles this encounter with her son. And note, this is not a conversation and this is not a dialogue for they are not engaging as peers. She is presenting a monologue, a sort of manifesto if you will, of wisdom she wants read into Solomon's intellectual record. As is the case with all wise and prudent women, it is apparent Bathsheba has prepared for this critical telling. This is no off the cuff, spontaneous, "I'm mad and I'm going to get this straight right now before you get in the house good" kind of encounter; quite the contrary. Observe how Bathsheba initiates the confrontation with her son. I am intentionally using the word confrontation with a very precise meaning or definition in mind. WordNet 3.0 @2006 by Princeton University defines confrontation as "a bold challenge" and "a focused comparison; a bringing together for a careful comparison".

It is clear from the rest of the text that Bathsheba has every intention of presenting a bold challenge and a focused comparison of right and wrong to her son. But that is not how she approaches him. She does not begin by fussing, yelling, screaming or crying. There is no hitting, smacking, pinching or throwing of shoes. There is no belt, no switch and no guilt trip. She does not begin by lamenting all she has gone through for him. She does not recount, in sickeningly gory detail, every minute of her 20 gazillion hours of labor with him. Bathsheba undoubtedly labored during Solomon's birth, but afterwards the memory of the pain was overshadowed by the joy of her child so there was no need to recount it. *"A woman when she is in travail hath sorrow, because her hour is come: but as soon as she is delivered of the child, she remembereth no more the anguish, for joy that a man is born into the world."* John 16:21. She doesn't mention the dirty diapers she changed or every time she sat up with him when he was sick. Bathsheba is not looking for thanks or affirmation from her son for the work that she has done as his mother. She is not even seeking recognition. No, she is far too wise and powerful to make the ultimate mistake in negotiation; to begin in anger. Instead, she begins in the manner of all great, skilled and successful negotiators-with commentary that can only generate an affirmative response. Bathsheba begins her talk, her confrontation with Solomon, with endearing words of love-maternal and confirming.

First she calls him her son. She does not begin with "I am your mother" rather she begins with "You are my son". That seemingly insignificant difference clarifies the fact that her focus is on him. This is a critical starting point because whatever else he has been, is now, or will become; whatever relationships he has had in the past or will forge later with others, nothing can change the fact that he is her son. Not only is he her son, but he came here as her son, and he will be her son forever. Even death cannot disintegrate the validity of that defining relationship. The love she has for him is an unearned, undeserved, unmerited and therefore priceless love. She loves him not because he is wise, not because he is king, not because he is rich and powerful. Her love is not conditioned on the temporal and fleeting trappings of his intellect, his status or his influence. She will love him if he loses his mind, his kingdom, his wealth and his power; and he knows it. She is pleased and proud of him and his accomplishments and achievements but they have no bearing on her love for him. She loves him because he is her son. This is a powerful position from which to begin a dialogue and because Bathsheba is a wise woman, she knows it.

Next she calls him the son of her womb. We are often reminded of how woman was created by God from the rib of man, thus making woman derivative. Here, in this brief phrase, "the son of my womb", Bathsheba illuminates how all men after Adam are derivative or taken from woman. The Apostle Paul's letter to the church at Corinth articulates the same point in I Corinthians 11:12 *"For as the woman is of the man, even so is the man also by the woman; but all things of God."* This is yet another example of the grace and mercy of God that He so wonderfully and beautifully perfected the biological reconciliation of man and woman. The first woman came out of a man's body and each subsequent man (or woman) comes out of the body of a woman. There is a kind of ongoing symbiosis in which each, the male and the female, is dependent upon the other and the wisest (and happiest!) among us intrinsically know, understand and embrace this union of opposites. In the recounting of this miraculous and obvious biological fact, Bathsheba further delineates the unique nature and quality of her love for her son and their relationship one to another.

This biological, mother-child relationship is not recounted to reduce or deny the love Solomon's father, David, felt for him. Rather Bathsheba stakes this claim and brings it to Solomon's conscious awareness as a reminder of the mystery they have shared from the magical moment of his conception and throughout his time in utero. She is not seeking his gratitude for carrying him through his gestation nor is she seeking his guilt for the inevitable pain she endured during his birth. No, Bathsheba simply wants Solomon to remember that she nurtured his existence when he was unable to do so himself.

She wants him to remember that their relationship is one that cannot be duplicated. She wants him to remember that he has inhabited only one womb-and it was hers. He was not adopted, he was not a foundling, he was not a slave given to her as a possession. He is the son of her womb and as such theirs is the temporal foundational relationship in his life. She began to know him before the umbilical cord was severed. Before he ever breathed his first independent breath, she already had begun the process of knowing him. As she felt her belly swell, as she felt his first quickening, as she saw the outline of his tiny feet pressed against her flesh, she knew then what it was to be literally "pregnant with purpose"; and she wants him to remember. That's why she was able to call him the son of my vows.

The son of my vows- is there any mother who has not held deep and secret hopes and dreams for her unborn child? Most often those dreams and hopes are so intense they are almost beyond words and can only be uttered in the spirit. In 1 Samuel 1:11 we have a chance to read the vow Hannah made secretly to God in her desperate plea for a child,

"And she vowed a vow, and said, O LORD of hosts, if thou wilt indeed look on the affliction of thine handmaid, and remember me, and not forget thine handmaid, but wilt give unto thine handmaid a man child, then I will give him unto the LORD all the days of his life, and there shall no razor come upon his head." Hannah had a clear and complete concept of her vow. Of course that doesn't mean she had a clear and complete concept of performing that vow. We may never know how hard it was for Hannah to leave her baby with the priest Eli. But Hannah knew in a way that only someone who yearns for something knows what it means to have a prayer answered. Unlike many women for whom pregnancy is not just natural but easy and too often regretted, Hannah was a woman who yearned for a son. Her heart ached for a child. And her hunger was so extreme that she was able to offer the future

sacrifice of that child just for the opportunity to conceive him, carry him, bear him, deliver him and care for him even if just for a few years. Hannah knew that her love for her son Samuel would remain inviolate throughout the totality of her life, for all the years after she left him with Eli at the temple. Hannah also knew what many modern mothers forget-or never really knew-the first three to five years are critical and the opportunity to imprint and instill beliefs and values will never be greater. Hannah had her time with her son Samuel and no doubt she cherished it and used the time wisely.

The scriptures tell us Hannah, like most mothers of her time nursed her child. The act of nursing involves more than just nourishment. It strengthens the psychological bond and transfers vital antibodies that protect and strengthen the child against disease. Nursing also speeds the healing of the uterus and has been viewed as a form of natural contraceptive. One thing is certain it forestalls a lot of other activities. Multitasking has its place in the modern world, but there are some things that deserve our undivided attention, for example the care of our children. Imagine how much information Hannah transferred to Samuel as she nursed him. And she didn't nurse him for a few days or weeks or months. In that time and even today in many parts of Africa, Asia and the Middle East, children are not weaned until they are 2 or 3 years old. Imagine how many prayers were uttered and how many hymns were sung while Hannah held Samuel in her arms and nursed him. She didn't have the option of sticking a bottle in his mouth and putting him in his crib so she could have some "me time". She knew her time with her child was short and she made the most of it. 1 Samuel 1:22-28 clearly illustrates her focused attention and the fulfillment of her promise or vow to the Lord. "*But Hannah went not up; for she said unto her husband, I will not go up until the child be weaned, and then I will bring him, that he may appear before the* LORD, *and there abide for ever. And Elkanah her husband said unto her, Do what seemeth thee good; tarry until thou have weaned him; only the*

LORD establish his word. So the woman abode, and gave her son suck until she weaned him. And when she had weaned him, she took him up with her, with three bullocks, and one ephah of flour, and a bottle of wine, and brought him unto the house of the LORD in Shiloh: and the child was young. And they slew a bullock, and brought the child to Eli. And she said, Oh my lord, as thy soul liveth, my lord, I am the woman that stood by thee here, praying unto the LORD. For this child I prayed; and the LORD hath given me my petition which I asked of him: Therefore also I have lent him to the LORD; as long as he liveth he shall be lent to the LORD. *And he worshipped the LORD there.*" (Emphasis mine)

Deuteronomy 6:5-9 articulates with specificity the job Hannah begged to undertake for her yet-to-be-conceived son. "*And thou shalt love the LORD thy God with all thine heart, and with all thy soul, and with all thy might. And these words, which I command thee this day, shall be in thine heart: And thou shalt teach them diligently unto thy children, and shalt talk of them when thou sittest in thine house, and when thou walkest by the way, and when thou liest down, and when thou risest up. And thou shalt bind them for a sign upon thine hand, and they shall be as frontlets between thine eyes. And thou shalt write them upon the posts of thy house, and on thy gates.*"

The critical nature of these biblical instructions are repeated hundreds of years later in the famous poem by William Ross Wallace, "*The Hand that Rocks the Cradle*".

> "Blessings on the hand of women!
> Angels guard its strength and grace,
> In the palace, cottage, hovel,
> Oh, no matter where the place;
> Would that never storms assailed it,
> Rainbows ever gently curled;
> For the hand that rocks the cradle
> Is the hand that rules the world.

Infancy's the tender fountain,
Power may with beauty flow,
Mother's first to guide the streamlets,
From them souls unresting grow–
Grow on for the good or evil,
Sunshine streamed or evil hurled;
For the hand that rocks the cradle
Is the hand that rules the world.

Woman, how divine your mission
Here upon our natal sod!
Keep, oh, keep the young heart
open Always to the breath of God!
All true trophies of the ages are
from mother-love impearled;
For the hand that rocks the cradle
is the hand that rules the world.

Blessings on the hand of women!
Fathers, sons, and daughters cry,
And the sacred song is mingled
with the worship in the sky—
Mingles where no tempest darkens,
rainbows evermore are hurled;
For the hand that rocks the cradle
is the hand that rules the world."

Remember that Bathsheba had already lost a son, in an incredibly painful and publicly humiliating way. Is there any doubt that she spent many, many hours in prayer for this son Solomon? Is there any doubt that she made manifold vows to God about this child? Is there any doubt that God heard her? No, no and no. We can conclude that because in 2 Samuel 12:25 we are told how Nathan the prophet responded to David's news of the birth of this child. *"And he sent by the hand of Nathan the prophet; and he called his name Jedidiah, because of the LORD."* Various interpretations of that scripture define Jedidah as "for the Lord's sake," "the Lord's Beloved," and "for Jehovah's or Yahweh's sake".

As we come to the end of this relatively simple declarative statement of Proverbs 31:2, we see the development of Bathsheba's confrontation, her "bold challenge" with her son. When she concludes with the phrase *"the son of my vows"* we can see some parts of the future she imagined for him. The imagination for his future encompassing his wisdom is displayed in the book of Proverbs; his philosophical intellect illuminated in Ecclesiastes and his amazing ability to establish transcendence between eroticism and spirituality in The Song of Solomon. Bathsheba's vows for her son were an illustration of her faith that God had not just forgiven her past sin with David, but that He was also willing to bless her and most importantly bless the son she had conceived with David. Like the rest of us as women, mothers, grandmothers, aunts, sisters and friends, Bathsheba prayed that her son would have the strength and the courage to accept and acknowledge his gifts and walk in them.

Bathsheba knew the obstacles when Solomon was born. She knew he was David's 30th son-not his first. When Solomon came into his kingdom he was not David's eldest surviving son. The eldest surviving son was Adonijah, the son of Haggith, David's 4th son. The scriptures carefully delineate all of David's male progeny, his sons, and the order of their birth and the names of their mothers. 2 Samuel 3:4. *"And the fourth, Adonijah the son of Haggith."* The Bible Encyclopedia translates the name Adonijah as *"My Lord is Jehovah"* so we know this man was not a bum; and, as the eldest surviving son, he had every reason to believe he should succeed David on the throne. But I think Bathsheba knew in her spirit, just as Nathan knew in the Spirit that Solomon, not Adonijah, was the one to continue and expand the kingdom. 1 Kings 1:11-37 shows this confirmation and coordination of spiritual insight between Bathsheba and Nathan. Now the following is a lengthy passage, but I think it's worth the time to read it.

"Wherefore Nathan spake unto Bathsheba *the mother of Solomon, saying, Hast thou not heard that Adonijah the son of Haggith doth reign, and David our lord knoweth it not? Now therefore come,* let me, I pray thee, give thee counsel, *that thou mayest save thine own life, and the life of thy son Solomon.* Go and get thee in unto king David, and say unto him, Didst not thou, my lord, O king, swear unto thine handmaid, saying, Assuredly Solomon thy son shall reign after me, *and he shall sit upon my throne? why then doth Adonijah reign? Behold,* while thou yet talkest there with the king, I also will come in after thee, and confirm thy words. *And Bathsheba went in unto the king into the chamber: and the king was very old; and* Abishag the Shunammite ministered unto the king. And Bathsheba bowed, and did obeisance unto the king. *And the king said, What wouldest thou? And she said unto him, My lord, thou swarest by the LORD thy God unto thine handmaid, saying, Assuredly Solomon thy son shall reign after me, and he shall sit upon my throne. And now, behold, Adonijah reigneth; and now, my lord the king, thou knowest it not: And he hath slain oxen and fat cattle and sheep in abundance, and hath called all the sons of the king, and Abiathar the priest, and Joab the captain of the host: but Solomon thy servant hath he not called .And thou, my lord, O king, the eyes of all Israel are upon thee, that thou shouldest tell them who shall sit on the throne of my lord the king after him. Otherwise it shall come to pass, when my lord the king shall sleep with his fathers, that I and my son Solomon shall be counted offenders.* And, lo, while she yet talked with the king, Nathan the prophet also came in. *And they told the king, saying, Behold Nathan the prophet. And when he was come in before the king, he bowed himself before the king with his face to the ground. And Nathan said, My lord, O king, hast thou said, Adonijah shall reign after me, and he shall sit upon my throne?*

For he is gone down this day, and hath slain oxen and fat cattle and sheep in abundance, and hath called all the king's sons, and the captains of the host, and Abiathar the priest; and, behold, they eat and drink before him, and say, God save king Adonijah. But me, even me thy servant, and Zadok the priest, and Benaiah the son of Jehoiada, and thy servant Solomon, hath he not called. Is this thing done by my lord the king, and thou hast not showed it unto thy servant, who should sit on the throne of my lord the king after him? Then king David answered and said, Call me Bathsheba. And she came into the king's presence, and stood before the king. And the king sware, and said, As the LORD liveth, that hath redeemed my soul out of all distress, Even as I sware unto thee by the LORD God of Israel, saying, Assuredly Solomon thy son shall reign after me, and he shall sit upon my throne in my stead; even so will I certainly do this day. Then Bathsheba bowed with her face to the earth, and did reverence to the king, and said, Let my lord king David live for ever. *And king David said, Call me Zadok the priest, and Nathan the prophet, and Benaiah the son of Jehoiada. And they came before the king. The king also said unto them, Take with you the servants of your lord, and cause Solomon my son to ride upon mine own mule, and bring him down to Gihon: And let Zadok the priest and Nathan the prophet anoint him there king over Israel: and* blow ye with the trumpet, and say, God save king Solomon. Then ye shall come up after him, that he may come and sit upon my throne; for he shall be king in my stead: and I have appointed him to be ruler over Israel and over Judah. *And Benaiah the son of Jehoiada answered the king, and said, Amen: the LORD God of my lord the king say so too.* As the LORD hath been with my lord the king, even so be he with Solomon, and make his throne greater than the throne of my lord king David.
(Emphasis mine)

Bathsheba didn't just pray a vow for her son, she remained vigilant to do anything and everything she could to assist Solomon's growth towards his telos. When Nathan came and offered her counsel about her son and his future, she had enough sense to listen and follow his advice. She took the risk to seek an unsolicited audience with the King. And when she got there and saw a younger woman there "ministering" to him, she didn't get an attitude and forget why she was there in the first place. After her gentle reminder of David's earlier promise, Bathsheba removed herself when Nathan arrived-and waited to be recalled into the presence of the King. And when David granted her wish, she graciously thanked him without any snide commentary, like "That's better!" Bathsheba nurtured Solomon and his gifts and his calling from his conception until his coronation. Solomon's famous wisdom, wealth and power transcend Judaism and Christianity. In the Qur'an Solomon is known as the famous Sulayman, which translates "man of peace".

No doubt knowing the quantity, quality and intensity of her prayer life and her vows for Solomon, Bathsheba did not hesitate to initiate a confrontation with him. When you pray for someone, continuously and without ceasing, from conception through coronation, the way wise mothers pray for their children, you know you have earned the right to offer sound counsel. When I reflect upon Solomon's wisdom in the light of what the scriptures tell us about Bathsheba I am reminded of an expression the Irish use to comment on the seemingly inexplicable conduct of children, "He didn't lick that off the ground".

CHAPTER 4 QUESTIONS

1. What do you think of Bathsheba's approach? Was the lovey-dovey stuff sneaky?

    _____

    _____

    _____

2. Could this loving approach to correction work with children today? Why or why not?

    _____

    _____

    _____

3. What do think of Bathsheba's reminding Solomon of his significance in her life?

    _____

    _____

    _____

4. Why is it important for us to be mindful of the impact of our life and our life decisions on others?

    _____

    _____

    _____

5. Do you think Bathsheba's prayers for Solomon were unusual in their intensity or effectiveness? How do you think the death of her first son affected her prayer life?

_____

_____

_____

6. Do you know any mothers today who seem as vigilant about their children as Bathsheba was of Solomon?

_____

_____

_____

7. If you observed such vigilance, what would you think of that mother, careful or crazy?

_____

_____

_____

8. What impact do you think Bathsheba's "interference" with the royal succession had on Solomon's status among his peers? Do you think Solomon cared what "the guys" thought about it?

_____

_____

_____

9. Do you think Solomon would have succeeded David without the intervention of Nathan and Bathsheba? Do you think she held her assistance over his head?

    _____

    _____

    _____

10. What can we learn from Bathsheba's style of involvement with her son and his response to it? How might we apply those lessons in the modern, fragmented world where youth rather than experience is revered?

    _____

    _____

    _____

CHAPTER 5

"You Need to Listen"

Pleasure can be intoxicating at any age.

What might Bathsheba be cautioning against in Proverbs 31: 3? What is the danger of promiscuity for young men? What is it that destroys kings? How are danger and destruction connected? Are her words a variation on the warning about the lust of the eye, lust of the flesh and the pride of life? And why are these warnings so seldom included in discussions on the biblical text of "The Virtuous Woman"?!

Proverbs 31:3 states *"Give not thy strength unto women, nor thy ways to that which destroyeth kings."* This two-fold instruction seems simple enough. So much so that one can easily imagine a dismissive and in-sincere affirmative response from the hearer. You know what I mean, like when you try to tell your kids something, something important, something vital even, but because they've heard it a thousand times before they roll their eyes, sign loudly and say, "Yeah, okay, okay, Mom." I'll use myself as a negative example. When I was away in college, my mother would send me care packages, which was great, but inside the packages were notes with her own unique hieroglyphic messages, "I love you" written as a drawing of an eye + a heart + the letter U., that sort of thing. All very cute, but interspersed along with the notes would also be questions, i.e., "Are you still saved?" and admonitions, i.e., "Remember what I taught you." This was in addition to my father's *daily* phone calls, which were great for quick cash, but also included questions like, "How's Daddy's princess?" and similar words of caution and concern "Be careful; Lord be with you." Of course, at the time, I found it all terribly tedious because well, it was so insultingly obvious and I'd heard it all before, ad nauseum.

Thankfully I was blessed with wise parents who truly could not have cared less that I found their commentary repetitive and boring. And I'm guessing that the adolescent me and the current crop of young people are not alone in this dismissive attitude about repetitive warnings and words of caution. Sadly it is a common occurrence across the spectrum of time; and the scary part is we don't always outgrow it. Too often we assume an inaccurate correlation based on a facile or surface truth, namely, that to hear something repeated is to both know *and* understand it.

It is an oft repeated statement, "knowledge is power" and it is; but that is just part of the truth. Just as the statement, "For we know all things work together for the good" is true, *but* it is true only in conjunction with a larger truth contained in the rest of that scripture, namely "for them that love God *and* are the called according to His purpose." So, in fact, all things in and of themselves do *not* work together for the good, nor is it "all good"; and wishing alone will not make it so in the absence of the rest of that scripture. Similarly, for knowledge to become power, that which is known must be understood. Just as all things can work together for the good under certain circumstances, certain conditions must also be met for knowledge to create power.

A related mistake is the assumption that things that are simple (because we've heard them a zillion times!) are also easy. In fact, many things that are simple are quite difficult. Example? The process of weight management is quite simple, namely eat less, exercise more, yet the fact that we in the United States just keep getting fatter and fatter is proof that this simple fact is anything but easy in its application. By the same token, hearing something often enough to be able to repeat it does not mean we have truly listened, nor does it mean we are beyond the need for reminders. We think hearing principles stated often enough to repeat them, verbatim, means we understand and can apply them. It's like the adage "the announcements have been read in your hearing; govern yourself accordingly". The statement makes sense, but the "govern yourself accordingly part" rarely happens. Yet we continue to think hearing equates to listening. No doubt Solomon thought the same incorrect thing when his mother confronted him. What she was telling him was certainly not new; the information was not obscure, and she, his father King David, and the prophet Nathan had undoubtedly told Solomon all of this many, many, many times before. His probable boredom with the repetition and his desire to get on with his life hardly seems unreasonable. Yet when we carefully examine this deceptively simple statement in verse 3, we see just how laden with wisdom it is. Fortunately for Solomon, Bathsheba, like many of our mothers, was not dissuaded about repeating important messages. Let her actions in this verse be a lesson to us.

<u>Strong's</u> Hebrew translation of the text is illuminating, so much so that it's worth a line-by-line, word-for-word examination. "*Give not thy strength unto women nor thy ways to that which destroyeth kings.*" In

Hebrew the verb "give" is translated "nathan (naw-than')" and implies give in its broadest sense as in "to put, or make". Look at how that broad definition in the Hebrew corresponds to current usage. Merriam-Webster's Online Dictionary's definition of give includes "make a present of, grant or bestow by formal action, put into the possession of another and provide by way of entertainment." (Remember the line from that old secular song by the Everly Brothers, "Here he comes, that's Cathy's clown"? It takes on a deeper and more sinister connotation when we get past the catchy melody and consider what it means to see a man's existence reduced to entertainment!)

Chayil (khah'-yil), Strong's Hebrew translation of "strength", includes "a force, wealth, strength, valor" or-you guessed it-"virtue". That ancient definition coincides with many aspects of the word's contemporary definitions offered in Merriam-Webster's Online Dictionary, specifically "a capacity for exertion or endurance, intensity or potency and the power to resist force or attack". As capacity implies finiteness or limits, this begs the question, how much strength can be given away before it is completely consumed? Bathsheba wanted Solomon to explore this vital question while he still had strength, intensity and "the power to resist force or attack."

Earlier, in Chapter 2 we examined the Hebrew translation and definition of *woman*. Ishshah (ish-shaw') *a woman, each, every female, wife, woman*; the irregular plural is nashiym (naw-sheem'), a woman. Interestingly this definition in Strong's Hebrew Dictionary does not offer a distinction between a woman who is a wife and a woman who is not. In this instance then, we can safely conclude that Bathsheba's concern for Solomon was not based on the marital or parental status of any particular woman. She was admonishing him to be conscious of the implicit power of any and all women. I don't think she gave this blanket warning because she was filled with self-loathing about herself and therefore, by extension, all other women. I think she offered this admonition because she knew first hand, the terrible consequences that can follow the almost irresistible lust that can arise between a man and a woman.

Bathsheba placed the responsibility for disciplined self-control squarely on Solomon's shoulders. She knew, almost instinctively and without the benefit of New Testament teachings that a man who cannot discipline his own flesh can never be the man God desires him to be. If we continue our line-by-line examination of Proverbs 31:3 I think Bathsheba's rationale will become even clearer to us.

"Give not thy strength unto women, nor thy ways to that which destroyeth kings." The word *way*, derek (deh'-rek), is defined in <u>Strong's Hebrew Dictionary</u> as *a road* or figuratively *a course of life* or *mode of action.* John 14:6 also speaks of the way. *"Jesus saith unto him, I am the way, the truth, and the life: no man cometh unto the Father, but by me."* In the secular world of words, Merriam Webster's Online Dictionary provides a fascinatingly consistent series of definitions for *way.* The Latin etymology or origin is "vehere", *to carry, via, way,* and from there we see the common derivatives, *a thoroughfare for travel* or *transportation from place to place; an opening for passage, a course of action, a characteristic, regular or habitual manner or mode of being, behaving or happening.*

Clearly Bathsheba is expanding her admonition beyond the rather common place warning about the perils of casual sexual encounters. She is talking about much more than the inevitable waning of physical strength and virility through poor choices and resulting dissipation. She is talking about the establishment of patterns of behavior, the unconscious creation of habits-*ways.* How much energy, strength and potency have each of us expended trying to break habits we willfully cultivated? Would we not spare others from the same wastefulness? And what more could we have done and accomplished with all that "extra" time we've spent trying to wean ourselves from things like murmuring and complaining, gossiping, back-biting, gluttony, rebelliousness and covetousness? Notice I didn't even mention our old Holiness standbys of bingo, cards, movies, dancing, drinking, smoking, drugging and sexual immorality.

The second segment of Bathsheba's parenthetical phrase speaks to the broader challenge of dissipation and wasteful, wanton living. She is speaking of those ways, openings, courses of actions, characteristics and habitual manners that are dangerous and destructive precisely because they appear so common place, so everyday, so innocent and innocuous at first blush. These seemingly innocent activities are tolerated and even encouraged in young men. Bathsheba wanted her son Solomon to be aware of the dangers of these common and widely accepted practices.

Even today we hear the excuses provided as a thinly veiled encouragement and inducement to presumptuous sin by young men in the colloquial axiom, "He's just sowing his wild oats". Yet that phrase has more prophetic truth than many of us know or care to acknowledge. The wild oat is a common tall plant, a weed, whose Latin name, Avena fatua, says it all. Avena is Latin for *oats* and fatua translates as *foolish, insipid* or *worthless*. Avena fatua is a pernicious weed that is difficult to kill and has been known for its uselessness since ancient times. The Encyclopedia of Word and Phrase Origins by Robert Hendrickson (Facts on File, New York, 1997) reports the expression to "sow wild oats" can be traced to the Roman comic Plautus in 194 B.C. The expression has been used consistently to refer to a young man wasting time, generally in prolific sexual activities or other forms of dissipation.

When we examine the definition and meaning of the word *dissipation*, in conjunction with what we know about the colloquial phrase "sowing wild oats", the conclusion of Bathsheba's warning comes into much clearer focus. Merriam-Webster defines dissipation as *wasteful expenditure, intemperate living; especially: excessive drinking: an act of self-indulgence; especially: one that is* not harmful: *an amusement. (Emphasis mine).* This is an interesting examination of the word dissipation, however we as saints of God and practitioners of Holiness know only too well that acts of self-indulgence, whether they involve excessive drinking or not, are anything but harmless amusements.

Make no mistake, we are not self-righteous, stiff-necked pretenders- or at least most of us aren't. Nor are we scamming ourselves or one another by acting as if we were "born saved"; hence we are not unaware of the ways of the world. We understand temptation and we know how easy it is to give in to our flesh and its desires. It's not something we heard about or something we read about. We know because *"all have sinned and fallen short of the glory of God."* Romans 3:23. Thankfully we know also that when we sin and fall short, if we confess, God's grace is quick to forgive us. But we do not presume on the grace of God nor do we accept these sins and shortcomings, in ourselves or others, and certainly not in our children, as harmless amusements. Romans 6:1 *"What shall we say then? Shall we continue in sin, that grace may abound?"* God forbid! Instead we know and we must instill in our children, regardless of their ages, the knowledge that we who are God's elect must keep our flesh and our instinct for self-indulgence under control. As we continue in Romans Chapter 6 we see not only the immediate danger of self-indulgence, but the long-term costs.

Romans 6:12-23 *"Let not sin therefore reign in your mortal body, that ye should obey it in the lusts thereof. Neither yield ye your members as instruments of unrighteousness unto sin: but yield yourselves unto God, as those that are alive from the dead, and your members as instruments of righteousness unto God. For sin shall not have dominion over you: for ye are not under the law, but under grace. What then? shall we sin, because we are not under the law, but under grace? God forbid. Know ye not, that to whom ye yield yourselves servants to obey, his servants ye are to whom ye obey; whether of sin unto death, or of obedience unto righteousness? But God be thanked, that ye were the servants of sin, but ye have obeyed from the heart that form of doctrine which was delivered you. Being then made free from sin, ye became the servants of righteousness. I speak after the manner of men because of the infirmity of your flesh: for as ye have yielded your members servants to uncleanness and to iniquity unto iniquity; even so now yield your members servants to righteousness unto holiness. For when ye were the servants of sin, ye were free from righteousness. What fruit had ye then in those things whereof ye are now ashamed? for the end of those things is death. But now being made free from sin, and become servants to God, ye have your fruit unto holiness, and the end everlasting life. For the wages of sin is death; but the gift of God is eternal life through Jesus Christ our Lord."*

Even without the spirit of discernment which accompanies the infilling of the Holy Ghost, our sister Bathsheba, one of the feminine ancestors of Jesus Christ, knew Solomon needed a clear and succinct warning about his *ways.* Contrary to the definition of dissipation offered in Merriam-Webster's Online Dictionary, Romans 6: 23 states emphatically that self-indulgence and careless sin is anything but harmless. This dire warning intersects perfectly with the scientific definition of dissipation used in the study of physics.

"Physics" is a Greek word which translated literally means the knowledge of nature. It is that branch of science focused on the discovery and characterization of the universal laws that control matter, energy, space and time. Physics is known as the "fundamental science" because chemistry, biology and other fields of science explore systems whose properties depend on the laws of physics. In physics, dissipation is defined much differently and with far greater precision than in Merriam-Webster.

Dissipation in physics is the idea or representation of a dynamical system by which important mechanical modes such as waves, lose energy over time, usually due to turbulence or friction. Now at first glance that seems overly technical, but when we break it down it really isn't that complex or beyond our keen. All things in this universe were created by God and therefore, by knowing God, on some level, we can begin, through careful, diligent and disciplined study to understand His creation, even if "through a glass darkly". So let us examine these concepts of waves and dissipation in physics, line-by-line and precept-by-precept.

A wave is a form of energy transfer from one place to another with minimal to zero displacement of the particles of the medium. A scriptural example of this is seen in Acts 2:1-4. *"And when the day of Pentecost was fully come, they were all with one accord in one place. And suddenly there came a sound from heaven as of a rushing mighty wind, and it filled all the house where they were sitting. And there appeared unto them cloven tongues like as of fire, and it sat upon each of them. And they were all filled with the Holy Ghost, and began to speak with other tongues, as the Spirit gave them utterance."* The in-filling of the Holy Ghost, both historically during the Day of Pentecost and in our services today, constitutes a move of God. The transfer of energy, Jesus Christ, the promised Comforter, from Himself to us, His believers, fits the definition of wave used in physics.

Another theological example of wave is set forth in Matthew 18:18-29 *" Verily I say unto you, Whatsoever ye shall bind on earth shall be bound in heaven: and whatsoever ye shall loose on earth shall be loosed in heaven. Again I say unto you, That if two of you shall agree on earth as touching any thing that they shall ask, it shall be done for them of my Father which is in heaven. For where two or three are gathered together in my name, there am I in the midst of them."*

When we as saints of God "touch and agree", we transfer energy with minimal to zero displacement of our particles. The promised confirmation of the effectiveness of the transfer of our collective energy across and between one another is verified in James 5:16 *"Confess your faults one to another, and pray one for another, that ye may be healed. The effectual fervent prayer of a righteous man availeth much"*.

Just from these few scriptures, we can see clearly how important a wave, or energy transfer is in the spiritual as well as the physical universe. So how do we explain the spiritual consequences of a dynamical system in which waves lose energy or can be weakened? A dynamical system is a mathematical formulation for a fixed rule that explains the time dependence of a point's position in it's ambient or surrounding space. Every dynamical system has a state established by a set of points in a state space. The evolution rule of the dynamical system is a fixed rule that is deterministic. It describes what future states can flow from the current state. In any given time interval *only one future state can flow from the current state.* (Emphasis mine). The scriptural equivalent of the deterministic aspect of the evolution rule of dynamical systems is clearly illuminated in Romans 6:23 *"For the wages of sin is death; but the gift of God is eternal life through Jesus Christ our Lord"*. What Bathsheba knew from her own sin of adultery with King David, his murder of her husband Uriah and the resulting, redemptive death of her first son with David, was that the one future state that can flow from a current state of sin is death. This is the Biblical example of a dynamical system. And even without knowledge of modern theories of physics, Bathsheba knew that dissipation or the loss of energy was one of the ways "that destroyeth kings".

Strong's Hebrew Dictionary defines *destroy*, machah (maw-khaw'), the root word of destroyeth, as *to stroke or rub; by implication, to erase; also to smooth (as if with oil), i.e. grease or make fat; also to touch.* Stroking, rubbing, erasing, smoothing, touching-all these action verbs describe forms of friction. This slow erosion of force through the friction of continuous contact with things that are ungodly, that is what Bathsheba was warning Solomon against; that is what destroys kings. Merriam-Webster's Online Dictionary definition of *destroy* is equally harsh; *to bring to a complete end the physical soundness, existence or usefulness of; to ruin the structure, organic existence, or condition of: to put out of existence: to neutralize, i.e., the moon* destroys *the light of the stars"*.

Is there anything sadder than a king who has been "neutralized"? Can we be surprised by the intensity of Bathsheba's concern for Solomon and his ways? Should we feel any less burdened when we see our sons, grandsons, brothers, nephews and cousins neutralized by sin and living beneath their station? Bathsheba's ancient warning merges with the definition of dissipation used in modern physics. Remember? *Dissipation in physics is the idea or representation of a dynamical system by which important mechanical modes such as waves, lose energy over time, usually due to turbulence or friction.* On some level, Bathsheba intrinsically knew the fixed rule of dynamical systems, namely that the wages of sin would always be death and would most often be paid in the future–with interest. In that same intuitive way, she knew that important mechanical modes or waves–the energy transferred across generations–would lose force over time through the turbulence or friction caused by repetitive exposure to and engagement in sin. While she did not possess the vocabulary to discuss and define these concepts in modern technical terms, the critical message she conveyed to Solomon says it all. We who are the mothers, grandmothers, sisters, aunts and cousins of young men today can afford to do no less. We must remind them of Bathsheba's simple admonition in Proverbs 31:3 *"Give not thy strength unto women, nor thy ways to that which destroyeth kings"*.

CHAPTER 5 QUESTIONS

Proverbs 31:3 states "*Give not thy strength unto women, nor thy ways to that which destroyeth kings.*"

1.   What is the danger of promiscuity, particularly for young men?

2.   Are there connections between danger and destruction? If so, what are they?

3.   Is it necessary to repeat admonitions and warnings to young people (and the rest of us)? Do you ever get tired of saying the same thing over and over? When should you stop?

4.   Is it enough to know you've been heard? How is hearing different from listening?

5. Bathsheba warns Solomon about protecting his "ways". Are we as concerned about the moral "ways" or habits of young men as we are about those of young women? Does God make this gender distinction?

    _____

    _____

    _____

6. Do we as women tolerate or encourage the sowing of wild oats in young men? What are the dangers of sowing wild oats, how might it lead to destruction?

    _____

    _____

    _____

7. How might the sowing of wild oats bring about destruction later in life? Might that be related to the warning of that old song, *God's Gonna' Separate the Wheat from the Tares?*

    _____

    _____

    _____

8. Do we think clearly enough about how our actions might lead to dissipation or the reduction of our strength and energy?

    _____

    _____

    _____

9. Is our collective dissipation or reduction of strength within the body of Christ reducing our ability to utilize the power of the Holy Ghost in our daily lives?

    _____

    _____

    _____

10. What can we do, individually and collectively, to re-vitalize our ourselves, intellectually (Proverbs 23:7, as a man thinketh so he is); physically (Romans 4:17, speaking those things that are not as thought they were); and spiritually (Matthew 17:21, but this kind does not go out except by prayer and fasting).

    _____

    _____

    _____

CHAPTER 6

"Who Are You Supposed To Be?!"

Sometimes young people forget themselves, who they really are and that their lives are not their own; that's why they need their parents to remind them. Here we see Bathsheba remind Solomon of both his status and his responsibilities.

It is not for kings, O Lemuel, it is not for kings to drink wine; nor for princes strong drink: Lest they drink, and forget the law, and pervert the judgment of any of the afflicted. Give strong drink unto him that is ready to perish, and wine unto those that be of heavy hearts. Let him drink, and forget his poverty, and remember his misery no more. Proverbs 31:4-7

In continuing from Proverbs 31:3's cautionary tale of waste, lust and dissipation, Bathsheba adds another dimension of advice and admonition to her son Solomon. As yet she has not introduced any discussion of the duties and attributes of the proverbial virtuous woman. Perhaps she still is preparing Solomon to recognize, appreciate and be worthy of finding such a woman. In any event, in verse 3 Bathsheba cautions in simple and direct terms against the practice of promiscuity so common in men, particularly those of prominence, power and wealth. She warns Solomon of the duality of danger and destruction and their traveling companions, dissolution and dissipation, through the deliberate wasting of time, energy and sexual passion.

Now Bathsheba expands her discussion to include the rationale and reason for abstinence from alcohol to her prohibitions against other popular, yet dangerous and ungodly practices. Bathsheba has many hopes and dreams for Solomon, whom she refers to in Proverbs 31:2 as *"the son of my vows"*. But above all else, Bathsheba wants Solomon to come to full consciousness about his place and purpose in the universe and to do that she knows she must approach her wise son with wisdom. Remember, Bathsheba learned the hard way how to handle her life and the men in it wisely and with deliberate forethought. Like many women in the world then and now, particularly in and around the Middle East, Bathsheba lived within the rigorous physical and sometimes violent constraints of a frequently inflexible, patriarchal social, religious and political environment. Nevertheless she bravely, and with conscious intent, deliberately held her thoughts, her words and most importantly her prayers as her own.

Stephen Bantu (Steve) Biko, a founder of South Africa's Black Consciousness Movement, died in police custody in Pretoria, South Africa, a martyr of the anti-aparteid struggle. In one of his most famous speeches delivered in 1971 at Cape Town, South Africa he succinctly stated "The most potent weapon in the hands of the oppressor is the mind of the oppressed". Centuries in advance of Stephen Biko's fight Bathsheba intrinsically knew the wisdom of his words. Those words were rephrased in the popular culture of the 1970's as "Free your mind and the rest will follow" culminating in Parliament Funkadelic's anthem album of a more vulgar title. This may seem an extreme connection to draw but I think it is instructive. As a woman not just of virtue, but of strength and power, Bathsheba, much like her scriptural sister Esther, does not conduct herself as one oppressed. She deliberately frees her mind and keeps it free, undoubtedly through prayer and fasting. Bathsheba brings the power and deliberateness of her free mind to her critical interactions with her son.

Bathsheba is keenly aware of at least part of Solomon's purpose. The fact that she may not be aware of the totality of his purpose is not a problem for her. What she does know is more than enough. Here again is a lesson in wisdom for us. None of us knows the totality of God's destiny for our sons, but what we do know is that they must be ready for His appearance, and like our sister Bathsheba, that should be more than enough to keep us motivated and on task. Bathsheba does not appear to feel any hesitancy in helping Solomon remember his divine destiny: he was, he is, and he always will be, destined to be king. Interestingly, Bathsheba acknowledges Solomon's kingly status, even before his coronation. This too is exemplary. Once, at the home-going of the mother of our pastor, Suffragan Bishop, Eugene Lundy, M.D. (and as an aside he is a real, bona fide, doctor, with a terminal degree from an accredited institution!)-but I digress. At this service, our then presiding prelate, the late Bishop Norman Wagner, made a brilliantly illuminating observation. He said that when his mother was making a cake, she always said she was making a cake, she never said she was making batter-even though all you could see in the bowl was batter. Before she cracked that first egg or took the butter out to come to room temperature or pulled out any of her mixing bowls, she knew she was making a cake.

That message was illuminating for me because I'm a bit of a cook and a baker myself. And no matter how big of a mess I make in the kitchen (and no matter how "concerned" my husband may look midway through the process), I know what I'm doing. I know when I'm making my Kahlua-iced German chocolate cake or my Sweet Potato Pie with the caramelized pecan topping. I know when I'm making my authentic Italian Lasagna with béchamel sauce or my mother's baked macaroni and cheese topped with buttered breadcrumbs. I know when I check my recipes, make out the shopping list, buy the groceries, organize the ingredients on the counter and plug in my trusty Kitchen Aid stand mixers. I know in my mind what I am making and what it will be-and I know it with a degree of certainty that cannot be shaken by what it looks like halfway through the process. It's a cook's insight that resonates with 1 John 3:2 *"Beloved, now are we the sons of God, and it doth not yet appear what we shall be: but we know that, when he shall appear, we shall be like him; for we shall see him as he is"*. I made a note to myself to repeat that message the next time one of my beloved sons behaved in a way that belied who they already were-the sons of God-even if it didn't *yet* appear that way.

The rest of Bathsheba's commentary in the following verses of Proverbs 31:5-7 fit neatly within the parameters of Solomon's kingship. This is a valuable lesson for us as we admonish the young men in our lives, especially when it seems as if they've forgotten who they are. We should be the ones to remind them of their kingship through their kinship with Jesus Christ. If Bathsheba thought Solomon with all his wisdom was at risk of forgetting his place in the scope of time, how much more do we need to remind the men in our lives, whether they are our fathers, husbands, brothers, uncles, sons, nephews, cousins or grandsons of their purpose? In the midst of seemingly endless repetition, it can be easy to forget that and instead focus on our frustrations with their past and/or present mistakes and missteps, "I'm sick of telling you'; or "I guess you're never going to learn"; or worse "You're just like ….!" And why are those comparisons so often negative?

Here's something else we can learn from Bathsheba. She clearly knew of the character challenges in Solomon's lineage, on both the right and the "wrong side of the blanket", but she fully expected him to transcend those challenges. Historical fun fact: The expression "the wrong side of the blanket" is an old English reference to illegitimacy. William the Conqueror, William I, King of England from 1066-1087, was known publicly as the bastard son of the Duke Robert I of Normandy. He was "born on the wrong side of the blanket" but his illegitimacy did not prevent his secular ascent to the throne of England. By the same token, illegitimacy is still a rampant (and still avoidable!) problem, but we cannot allow children conceived in such circumstances to view it as an insurmountable obstacle.

But back to the point, Bathsheba was not a geneticist and probably never had heard anything about the nurture versus nature controversy, but I don't think she would have seen it as a dichotomous "either/or" kind of thing. I believe Bathsheba would have known intrinsically that this was a diunital "both/and" kind of thing. She knew whether nature and/or nurture, genetics and/or environment-all things, must bow before the will of God. I think Bathsheba knew it was incumbent upon Solomon just as it is for the rest of us, to come into perfect obedience to the Word and the Will and the Way of God in order for destiny to be fulfilled.

It is not for kings, O Lemuel, it is not for kings to drink wine; nor for princes strong drink: Lest they drink, and forget the law, and pervert the judgment of any of the afflicted.

Bathsheba continues to speak to Solomon about the need for discipline and self-control in all aspects of his life. She doesn't just tell him "Don't drink!" She also doesn't say, "Promise Mommy you'll never,

ever drink!" Bathsheba knows such promises are easily broken, especially without reason to support them; this maybe why Bathsheba feels the need to explain the risk of alcohol consumption for kings and all men of destiny. *"Lest they drink, and forget the law, and pervert the judgment of any of the afflicted."* Bathsheba wants Solomon to grasp the totality of his "raison d'etre", a French phrase, translated "reason for existence".

Solomon has not been imbued with gifts for his own pride and pleasure any more than they have been bestowed for the pride and pleasure of his parents. He has a greater purpose, namely to remember the law and to judge the people righteously. Two ancient axioms come to mind when considering Bathsheba's wise counsel to her son. One warns, "Power corrupts and absolute power corrupts absolutely". The second states, "When a fish stinks, it starts at the head". Bathsheba as both the wife and the mother of kings knows how much power a king wields, and the destruction that can come from its corruption and abuse. She also knows that when the king (or the husband) fails to follow the leading of the Lord, the people, the family, suffer. Bathsheba wants Solomon to understand his purpose is to judge the people wisely and righteously. While Solomon apparently heard his mother, it appears he did not pass her wise counsel on to his son Rehoboam. Rehoboam was the last king of the united monarchy of Israel and the first king of Judah. Long after his grandmother Bathsheba's warnings to his father Solomon, Rehoboam's arrogant abuse of the people led to the division of the powerful kingdom he inherited.

2 Chronicles 10:6-11. *"And king Rehoboam took counsel with the old men that had stood before Solomon his father while he yet lived, saying, What counsel give ye me to return answer to this people? And they spake unto him, saying, If thou be kind to this people, and please them, and speak good words to them, they will be thy servants forever. But he forsook the counsel which the*

old men gave him, and took counsel with the young men that were brought up with him, that stood before him. And he said unto them, What advice give ye that we may return answer to this people, which have spoken to me, saying, Ease somewhat the yoke that thy father did put upon us? And the young men that were brought up with him spake unto him, saying, Thus shalt thou answer the people that spake unto thee, saying, Thy father made our yoke heavy, but make thou it somewhat lighter for us; thus shalt thou say unto them, My little finger shall be thicker than my father's loins. For whereas my father put a heavy yoke upon you, I will put more to your yoke: my father chastised you with whips, but I will chastise you with scorpions."

2 Chronicles 10:19 *"And Israel rebelled against the house of David unto this day"*.

Bathsheba's admonition to Solomon illuminates her insight into future circumstances within her own family and acts as a pre-cursor to the Apostle Paul's New Testament writings to the church at Corinth. *"All things are lawful unto me, but all things are not expedient: all things are lawful for me, but I will not be brought under the power of any"*. 1 Corinthians 6:12. And further, *"All things are lawful for me, but all things are not expedient: all things are lawful for me, but all things edify not."* I Corinthians 10:23. In both instances we see that often more than blanket prohibitions are called for; sometimes we are called upon to think so that we can make not just good choices, but the best choices. Sometimes there is more than right or wrong; there is good, better and best.

Years ago when we were preparing our twins for their rites of passage, our pastor was kind enough to meet with them monthly for almost an entire year to review scriptures and science, specifically the impact of mitochondrial DNA strains on the study of evolution. (And no, I did not understand 99% of the conversation–but that's not the point!) What I found intriguing was the little ditty he recited to them at the conclusion of each meeting. "Good, better, best, never let it rest, 'til your good is better and your better best." He did not comment on how busy he was as a pastor, or how knowledgeable he was as a cardiologist. He did not comment on the challenging nature of their study or the fact that they were just 12 years old. The analysis was not comparative; it was specific, and as such, good was not enough. Dictionary.com offers concise definitions of good, better and best. Good is "*satisfactory in quality;*" Better is "*of superior quality;*" and Best is "*the highest quality…surpassing all others.*"

Bathsheba knew her son was smart, she was his mother! It's nice when other people tell us how smart our sons are, but really, shouldn't we be the first to know that?! And beyond the knowing, shouldn't we be the first to speak that into our sons' hearing, daily?! Bedtime at our house was fiercely rigid when the boys were small. They tease us now about how they didn't know there was an eight o'clock at night until they went to school and heard other kids talking about it! But every night, after their bath, prayers, Bible reading and Good-Night kisses, we would turn out the light and the last thing we would say was "You are the smartest, most wonderful little boys in the whole world and Mommy and Daddy are blessed and thankful to be your parents." Charles and I already knew they were smart and special and we knew it was our job to make sure they knew it too. Bathsheba also knew how smart Solomon was, but at this point she's not tucking him in at night. She's not talking to him as her infant or toddler son. She's not talking to him as her school-aged son or her teenager. At this point, Bathsheba is speaking to Solomon as a grown man and she wants to be certain he knows what is expected of him.

She knows Solomon has the power to fool around with various women and drink and party and carouse. She also knows he always will have a willing entourage or as they say in the vernacular a "crew" or a "posse" at the ready, happy to "kick it" with him. But Bathsheba wants Solomon to be conscious consistently of his purpose; she wants him to make good, sound choices. She isn't asking him to "be good" just to please her, because she knows that is a short-term incentive. She wants him to be better than good. She wants him to think about his purpose more than she wants him to think about her. Thinking of her and wanting to please her might drive Solomon to be good, but more than his mother's approval is necessary if his best is to be achieved. Bathsheba wants Solomon to think because she knows that in the midst of his intellect lies the incentive to reach beyond what is comfortable to achieve what is right, what is pleasing to the Lord; that is the best.

God wants us to utilize fully all his gifts and benefits, including the ability to intellectually analyze our options and choices. When Paul says all things are legal, he is underscoring the fact that we, the New Testament Church, the Redeemed of the Lord, are in the dispensation of grace and we are not bound by the laws of the Old Testament. Yet, as is the case with all freedoms, spiritual and secular, there are attendant responsibilities of thought and analysis. Just because something is free and available to me does not mean that it is good for me. Or put another way, everything I'm big enough to do, don't need to be done! The children of Israel complained bitterly in the wilderness, not just because they wanted more than manna and yearned for leeks. I think they also yearned for freedom from responsibility, that's why they wanted to return to Egypt. When we are enslaved, either physically, intellectually or spiritually we have all kinds of excuses for sub-standard performance. Whether its "Massa won't let me be free" or "my crack genie won't let me be free" or "my mind won't let me forget and be free" or "my flesh won't let me forgive and be free"; in each of these, we only need apply the blood of Jesus and the infilling of the Holy Ghost for Truth to be revealed and freedom received. John 8:32 *"And ye shall know the truth, and the truth shall make you free."* John 8:36 *"If the Son therefore shall make you free, ye shall be free indeed."*

Bathsheba was not one of the Redeemed. She did not have the power of the Holy Ghost nor did her son Solomon. Yet in these few verses of Proverbs 31 we see that Bathsheba is admonishing her son to walk in the freedom and the fullness of his destiny. She is not asking him to please her, she is asking him to please God. This is yet another reason neither Bathsheba nor Solomon is concerned about how others may view their relationship or her influence in his life. In asking him to please God and to utilize his enormous intellectual gifts to do so, Bathsheba concludes this segment of the chapter with these telling lines *"Give strong drink unto him that is ready to perish, and wine unto those that be of heavy hearts. Let him drink, and forget his poverty, and remember his misery no more"*.

Again, she is not relying on a blanket prohibition against drinking. Bathsheba even offers instances in which drinking may be in order, but none of these conditions apply to her son! Is Solomon ready to perish? Is he of heavy heart? Is he stricken with a poverty so crippling that he is miserable and needs to forget? No, no and again I say no; Solomon has no such excuse to drink. Rather than harangue our sons with yet more arguments against drinking, perhaps we need to consider Bathsheba's approach. Perhaps we need to ask our sons the same hard questions, but in more modern language. "Are you so broke down that you cannot face your life and your circumstances? Are you so weak that your heart is heavy? Are you so ineffectual as a child of God, as a person and as a man that you have no ideas or insights on your situation? Is your situation, dire though it may be, so hopeless that prayer and meditation provide no solace leaving drinking as your only release?"

Granted, we all have moments when we may feel discouraged or even (momentarily) defeated, but we absolutely cannot give in to that and we certainly cannot allow our sons to give into it. Giving in can become a habit too easily, and when we justify or validate that habit in our sons, we might as well psychologically castrate them. If we believe our sons are in fact the sons of God, then we have to encourage them to stand rather than enable them to fall. We can never make the mistake of excusing poor performance in our sons because we respect them too much for that. At this point of potential discouragement and weakness, Bathseba can point her son Solomon to the writings of his father David in Psalm 24. *"The earth is the LORD's, and the fulness thereof; the world, and they that dwell therein. For he hath founded it upon the seas, and established it upon the floods. Who shall ascend into the hill of the LORD? or who shall stand in his holy place? He that hath clean hands, and a pure heart; who hath not lifted up his soul unto vanity, nor sworn deceitfully. He shall receive the blessing from the LORD, and righteousness from the God of his salvation. This is the generation of them that seek him ,that seek thy face, O Jacob. Selah. Lift up your heads, O ye gates; and be ye lift up, ye everlasting doors; and the King of glory shall come in. Who is this King of glory? The LORD strong and mighty, the LORD mighty in battle. Lift up your heads, O ye gates; even lift them up, ye everlasting doors; and the King of glory shall come in. Who is this King of glory? The LORD of hosts, he is the King of glory. Selah."*

It is never too soon to tell our sons to sit up straight and to hold their heads up. For those of us blessed to have given birth to African-American sons, this is an especially crucial lesson. Much like our biblical sister Esther, we are living as the descendants of slaves and sojourners in a strange land. We must caution our sons to carry themselves not in accordance of the world's view of them, but God's view. When our twins Charles and Damon were at Princeton, one of the many, many, many complaints several university officials expressed to us about them was that they were too "arrogant". And the evidence? "They walk around campus with their heads up." (Yeah, weird huh?) While my husband asked for the statement to be repeated–just to make sure we heard it correctly, neither of us was truly shocked. Presenting oneself with confidence can be disconcerting for lots of people for a variety of reasons; and it can be tempting for our sons, regardless of their racial, ethnic or socio-economic background, to move through the world with a posture of defeat. Yet presumptive defeat and surrender is not pleasing to God. We must remind our sons daily that if the Lord be for you, and we know that He is, He is more than the world against you!

CHAPTER 6 QUESTIONS

1. Is abstinence from alcohol still relevant? What about the argument that Jesus' first miracle was turning water into wine at the wedding feast?

   _____

   _____

   _____

2. Do you think Bathsheba intentionally withheld some of what she knew or believed about Solomon's future? What is the difference, if any, between knowing and believing?

   _____

   _____

   _____

3. Was Bathsheba wise in keeping her own counsel about Solomon or was she trying to manipulate him into doing what she wanted? If your motives are "right", is manipulation still wrong?

   _____

   _____

   _____

4. What do you think of Stephen Biko's statement that the mind of the oppressed is the most potent weapon of the oppressor? How might such a statement be relevant to mothers of both Bathsheba's time and ours?

   _____

   _____

   _____

5.   1 John 3:2 is an example of transcendence; it shows us the future state while we are yet in the present. "Beloved, *now are* we the sons of God, but it does not yet appear what we *shall be*. But we know when He shall appear, we shall be like Him." How can we apply that sense of transcendence when we deal with our sons?

_____

_____

_____

6.   How likely are we to draw negative conclusions and comparisons about our sons, "You're just like…"? Do you think those comments please God? How can we do a better job of encouraging our sons?

_____

_____

_____

7.   Bathsheba knew of Solomon's lineage and the challenges it presented, yet even without the power of the Holy Ghost, she didn't seem to believe he was limited by that. Do we really believe we can move past our family history or even the marital status of our parents when we were conceived? Are we sharing the power of that belief with our children.

_____

_____

_____

8.   Bathsheba does not rely on blind obedience in her advice to Solomon about drinking. She essentially asks him to think about his responsibilities and his status and then make a decision about drinking. Does this approach make sense to you? How

confident are you in your sons' ability to think and form sound decisions?

_____

_____

_____

9. When Bathsheba essentially says that drinking is for impotent, ineffective losers, is she merely trying to manipulate Solomon or do you think she really believes drinking is okay for people who cannot handle the complexities of their lives? Would you ever use such an approach with your own son?

_____

_____

_____

10. Do we encourage our children to think about their decisions or do we teach them to rely exclusively on prayer? How can we help them achieve balance between Proverbs 3:5 "Trust in the Lord with all thine heart and lean not unto thine own understanding" and Proverbs 23:7 "For as he thinketh in his heart, so is he"?

_____

_____

_____

CHAPTER 7

"What Are You Supposed To Be Doing?!"

Bathsheba turns this question around. Instead of focusing on Solomon's behavior, she helps him focus on his responsibilities. I think this is a good tactic, one definitely worth repeating!

"Open thy mouth for the dumb in the cause of all such as are appointed to destruction. Open thy mouth, judge righteously, and plead the cause of the poor and needy."

Proverbs 31: 8-9

We are coming to the culmination of Bathsheba's admonition and advice to her son before delineating the now famous attributes of the virtuous woman. I think Bathsheba felt her admonition and advice to Solomon was essential so he could be conscious and worthy when he met that virtuous woman. In the church today, it often appears as though the problem is not the lack of virtuous women nor of worthy and virtuous men. Rather, the challenge seems to be a mutual lack of conscious awareness of virtue. We who are mothers have to help our sons and our daughters grow in wisdom and discernment so that when they encounter virtue, they can recognize and value it. So before waxing eloquent on the potential virtues of women, Bathsheba works on helping Solomon to become worthy of that "good thing" as foretold with promise earlier in Proverbs. "*Whoso findeth a wife findeth a good thing, and obtaineth favour of the Lord.*" Proverbs 18:22

So, moving on, in verse one of Proverbs 31 we see validation of Bathsheba's words as prophecy. "*The words of king Lemuel, the prophecy that his mother taught him.*" In the second verse, we see another reflection of "Oneness" in the union of Bathsheba's intellectual, physical and spiritual knowledge of Solomon. "*What, my son? and what, the son of my womb? and what, the son of my vows?*" In the third verse, having already confirmed her unconditional love—without ever needing to say the word – she warns Solomon about a common (and what she may have viewed as a generational) curse or hereditary weakness. "*Give not thy strength unto women, nor thy ways to that which destroyeth kings.*" She goes on in verse 4 to layer warnings about drinking on top of her foundational warning about promiscuity. "*It is not for kings, O Lemuel, it is not for kings to drink wine; nor for princes strong drink.*" Verse 5 finds Bathsheba moving further to explain why drinking presents such a serious danger. "*Lest they drink, and forget the law, and pervert the judgment of any of the afflicted.*" In verses 6 and 7, Bathsheba clarifies the linkage between drinking and desolation. "*Give strong drink unto him that is ready to perish, and wine unto those that be of heavy hearts. Let him drink, and forget his poverty, and remember his misery no more."*

Much like a symphony builds to a crescendo in each movement, here we see Bathsheba's words of prophecy to her son build to the point of initial climax when she explains the beginning of the "why". Already she has clarified the "who", namely, her son Solomon; and the "what", specifically the need for discipline and self-control. This upcoming "why" is a further reflection of the perfection of "Oneness" for without a "why", the "who" and the "what" are inherently incomplete, their purpose obscured. In verses 8 and 9 Bathsheba brings the crescendo to the conclusion of this first and critical component of the chapter, the part dealing with Solomon's preparedness, with these words *"Open thy mouth for the dumb in the cause of all such as are appointed to destruction. Open thy mouth, judge righteously, and plead the cause of the poor and needy"*.

How many times have we looked at our children and examined the gap between their promise and their performance? And in how many of those times have we either thought – or actually asked – the quintessential question, "What are you supposed to be doing?!! Bathsheba presented a similar inquiry to her son by moving from a point of inquiry to a point of declaration. She doesn't ask him what he is doing; she can see that for herself. And even though she clearly is far from pleased by what she sees, she doesn't question him about it. Instead, she articulates what she knows he is supposed to be doing. She makes what is known grammatically as a declarative statement. Dictionary. com describes declarative as an adjective, defined as "serving to declare, make known, or explain." So when she tells him, "Open thy mouth for the dumb in the cause of all such as are appointed to destruction. Open thy mouth, judge righteously, and plead the cause of the poor and needy", she is explaining his purpose to him. She is making it known to him. She is serving to declare.

And what exactly does it mean to declare? Dictionary.com describes declare as a verb and it is defined as follows: "to make known or state clearly, esp. in explicit or formal terms; to announce officially, proclaim; to state emphatically; to manifest, reveal, show; to make due statement of, esp. goods for duty or income for taxation; to make (a dividend) payable." This secular definition of declare is intriguing, because it highlights the fullest meaning of the word.

Essentially, once something is declared, then something is owed. Here's an example. As many of you know, Charles and I love to travel. When our sons were younger we traveled with them for educational purposes. We strongly believe all children, but especially black children, benefit tremendously by seeing themselves in a broader, global perspective. Once our sons became adults however Charles and I continued to travel; but now it's just for fun, and at the risk of sounding truly slovenly, rarely do we do anything constructive, much less educational. We just walk around, sleep-a lot!-and of course eat far too much.

But back to the point of declare. On every return flight to the States, there is always a declaration form to be completed. On this form, everyone entering the U.S., whether as citizens or "aliens", must declare items being brought into the country. U.S. citizens must declare all purchases made while abroad if those purchases exceed a certain dollar amount; because if so, a duty or tax must be paid. And here's a critical and clarifying fact… the amount owed escalates based on the declared value! Only one form needs to be filled out per family. I'm always the one who completes the form-because I have beautiful penmanship. Charles, as the head of household, signs the form, thereby validating its accuracy-and his accountability- before turning it over to U.S. Customs. Because I know he trusts me, and because I know U.S. Customs does random checks of luggage, complete with drug-sniffing dogs, like my sister Bathsheba, I make it my business to know what everyone in our household has "to declare". Here's another critical and clarifying fact, the payment of duty or tax is not merely a secular form of revenue stream for governments. Spiritually, a duty or tax is also owed and the amount owed also varies based on value. This biblical fact is evidenced in Luke 12:48, *"For unto whomsoever much is given, of him shall be much required: and to whom men have committed much, of him they will ask the more"*.

We all have heard this adage, this maxim many, many times; even though we might not be able to recite its source, chapter and verse. But while we may be well acquainted with this verbiage, (a manner of expressing oneself with words) that may be all we have, a mere acquaintance. What does this word of warning really mean? Matthew Henry's <u>Whole Bible Commentary</u> offers the following detailed analysis:

What an aggravation it would be of their sin and punishment that they knew their duty, and did not do it (v. 47, 48): That servant that knew his lord's will, and did it not, shall be beaten with many stripes, shall fall under a sorer punishment; and he that knew not shall be beaten with few stripes, his punishment shall, in consideration of this, be mitigated. Here seems to be an allusion to the law, which made a distinction between sins committed through ignorance, and presumptuous sins (Lev. 5:15, etc.; Num. 15:29, 30), as also to another law concerning the number of stripes given to a malefactor, to be according to the nature of the crime, Deut. 25:2, 3.

Now, (1.) *Ignorance of our duty is an extenuation of sin.* He that knew not his lord's will, through carelessness and neglect, and his not having such opportunities as some others had of coming to the knowledge of it, and did things worthy of stripes, he shall be beaten, because he might have known his duty better, but with few stripes; his ignorance excuses in part, but not wholly. Thus through ignorance the Jews put Christ to death (Acts 3:17; 1 Co. 2:8), and

Christ pleaded that ignorance in their excuse: They know not what they do.

(2.) *The knowledge of our duty is an aggravation of our sin:* That servant that knew his lord's will, and yet did his own will, shall be beaten with many stripes. God will justly inflict more upon him for abusing the means of knowledge he afforded him, which others would have made a better use of, because it argues a great degree of willfulness and contempt to sin against knowledge; of how much sorer punishment then shall they be thought worthy, besides the many stripes that their own consciences will give them! Son, remember. Here is a good reason for this added: To whomsoever much is given, of him shall be much required, especially when it is committed as a trust he is to account for. *Those have greater capacities of mind than others, more knowledge and learning, more acquaintance and converse with the scriptures, to them much is given, and their account will be accordingly.* (Emphasis mine)

How wise of Bathsheba, an Old Testament ancestor of Jesus Christ, to have had this insight without the benefit of the discerning power of the Holy Ghost! She knew her son had been gifted beyond measure with good looks, intelligence, education, wisdom and wealth. She knew those gifts were valuable, and that because of that value, he would be held accountable. She completed his declaration form and listening to her state it was the spiritual equivalent of a signature.

So let's review the elements that Bathsheba declared to Solomon in verses 8 and 9. *"Open thy mouth for the dumb in the cause of all such as are appointed to destruction. Open thy mouth, judge righteously, and plead the cause of the poor and needy."*

By examining the lexicon, we can obtain a deeper understanding of the words in this text. And by understanding the individual words, we gain a deeper knowledge of the entire text or message. We don't all use the formal terminology; "lexicon: the vocabulary of a particular language, field, social class, person, etc."; but informally, we reference it. Here's an example. You know how when the doctor begins using technical medical terms, we'll often respond, "In plain English please". Or when a lawyer gives a technical analysis of a case, we'll often ask, "So what exactly does that mean?" Or when we hear folks talking about "the club", we sometimes have to guess at their socioeconomic level to know if they mean a nightclub or a country club. Or— and this may be the best example—sometimes when we listen (or eavesdrop!) on our kids speaking with their friends, often we don't have a clue what they mean! In each of those instances, we are in the dark, because we aren't familiar with the "lexicon: the vocabulary of a particular language, field, social class, person, etc." That's why examining the lexicon of the scriptures is so critical; it shows adherence to sound biblical advice. *"Study to shew thyself approved unto God, a workman that needeth not to be ashamed, rightly dividing the word of truth."* 2 Timothy 2:15. It isn't enough to just read the Word; the Word is to be studied, so that we can handle it with accuracy and precision.

So back to verse 8. *Open thy mouth for the dumb in the cause of all such as are appointed to destruction.* The Hebrew word for *Open* is pathach (paw-thakh), defined as "to open wide; specifically to loosen, begin, plough, carve". And *mouth*, peh (peh) references the mouth as a means of blowing, either literally or figuratively, but with special emphasis on speech. From those first two words of the verse, we see Bathsheba's declaration to Solomon that he open wide, loosen his mouth and blow. She's telling him, essentially, don't stumble, mumble or garble your words – speak up! And for whose benefit? *For the dumb*, illem (il-lame) the speechless, *in the cause*, duwn (doon), meaning judgement, strife, cause, suit, plea or sentence *of all such as are appointed*, ben (bane) as in a son or builder of the family name or of any literal or familial relationship such as a grandson, a subject, a nation, or a quality or condition, *to destruction*, chalowph (khal-ofe) surviving; by implication orphans. Bathsheba declares Solomon's duty, his spiritual "tax", is to use his gifts and callings to speak for those who cannot speak for themselves. She declares his obligation to interject himself, his strength, his wisdom, his influence into the conflict on behalf of the defenseless, those who would otherwise be destroyed.

Verse 9 equally is direct in its declaration. *Open thy mouth, judge righteously, and plead the cause of the poor and needy.* What's the duty articulated here? Again, we go to the lexicon, this time to examine *judge*, shaphat (shaw-fat), to pronounce sentence, to vindicate or punish, to govern, to litigate. And he must do so *righteously*, tsedeq (tseh-dek), the natural, moral or legal right, seeking equity and that which is just and right. He must do this *and plead*, diyn (deen), with a straight course-no deviation, *the cause of the poor*, aniy (aw-nee), those who are depressed-either in their minds or their circumstances; those who are afflicted, lowly, humble, needy or poor; *and needy*, ebyown (eb-yone), the destitute and the beggars.

Bathsheba is taking no chances with this element of her message to her son. She is crisp and crystal clear in her instructions. He is to judge-whether that entails vindication or punishment-and he is to do so righteously. Dictionary.com defines the verb vindicate as follows: "to clear from an accusation… to uphold… to defend against opposition". It cites under Roman and Civil Law "to regain possession, under claim of title of property through legal procedure, or to assert one's right to possession". Punish is defined as "to subject to pain, loss, confinement, death, etc., as a penalty for some offense, transgression, or fault."

Bathsheba knew intuitively that long after her death her son would still be on the throne – still tasked with the responsibility of judgment. She knew people would try to use their influence, their contacts, their money, and yes, their beauty to affect his judgment; to coerce him to heap punishment on some and vindicate others, without regard to merit. She wasn't worried about his wisdom, his ability both to look and to see beyond the obvious, the surface, or the superficial. She was confident of his ability to recognize illusion and deceptive thinking. This isn't merely a biblical challenge. Even today we see the challenge of illusory and deceptive thinking all the time and often comment on it, evidenced for example when we say things like, "Umph…She must think she's cute!" And of course, the unstated accompanying thought is "but she ain't!". But while Bathsheba knew Solomon had wisdom, she knew that wasn't sufficient for the judgment he was called to perform. That's why she admonished Solomon to righteous judgment.

Righteous is an adjective defined as, "characterized by uprightness or morality, morally right or justifiable, virtuous, absolutely genuine or wonderful". Notice that even in the secular definition offered by Dictionary.com, righteous is not equivalent to legal. Just as we know that everything that glitters ain't gold, everything that's legal is not righteous! Even as she lived under the law, Bathsheba knew the law, whether that brought down by Moses from Mount Sinai or the codified (written) law of man, held inherent limitations. Even before the advent of Jesus, Bathsheba was advocating for that which could only be described as "absolutely wonderful". Her admonition for righteousness was a precursor of the righteousness of Christ, of which His mercy is an integral component. The idea of righteousness as that which is "absolutely wonderful" is an essential requirement for Solomon's capacity to *"plead the cause of the poor and needy"*. That capacity is part of what is "absolutely wonderful" and so Christ-like; when the powerful intercedes for the powerless, the poor and the needy, that is a form of righteousness. I think that is what most of us want for our sons, a genuine and sincere desire to not just help themselves, but to help intercede for others as well. And if we want that, we must declare it to them.

Bathsheba's declaration for her son left no room for misunderstanding. She knew she had to be firm, because a failure to communicate would spell dire consequences for Solomon whom she so dearly loved. She was not willing to risk his potential punishment for noncompliance on her assumption that he already knew what to do. Undoubtedly, Bathsheba was certain Solomon previously had been told these things. Given Solomon's status in the palace as the son of the king, the product of that king's union with his favorite wife, a beautiful and brilliant young man, it is inconceivable that he would not have received years of sound instruction. Along with his regular tutors, he most likely received individual instruction from Nathan, the prophet, and probably a word or two from his father, King David. Granted, David had many sons, and probably wasn't able to spend a lot of time consistently with any of them individually, but how could he have been so willing to designate Solomon as his heir unless he knew something about him. I mean really, do we believe Bathsheba was *that* good?

Bathsheba knew Solomon had come of age in the palace, the son of a king, surrounded with wealth, tradition and instruction. Most importantly, Bathsheba knew Solomon ultimately would be held responsible for the proper and beneficial use of all of it. She held a spiritual anticipation of the apostle's prophetic words in Luke 12:48, *"For unto whomsoever much is given, of him shall be much required: and to whom men have committed much, of him they will ask the more"*. As this first movement of Proverbs 31's symphony comes to crescendo, Bathsheba makes a clear, deliberate declaration to her son, *"Open thy mouth for the dumb in the cause of all such as are appointed to destruction. Open thy mouth, judge righteously, and plead the cause of the poor and needy"*.

CHAPTER 7 QUESTIONS

1. What are you supposed to be doing! Have you ever asked your kids that question? Why —was it a real or rhetorical question?

   _____

   _____

   _____

2. *"Whoso findeth a wife findeth a good thing, and obtaineth favour of the Lord"*. Prov. 18:22. Are mothers today encouraging their sons to find that "good thing"? Should we be?

   _____

   _____

   _____

3. Do you think virtue is rarer today or is there a lack of conscious awareness of the existence and nature of virtue?

   _____

   _____

   _____

4. Are parents, especially mothers, doing enough to help develop virtue in their sons? Are we devoting the same amount of energy developing virtue in our sons as we are with our daughters?

   _____

   _____

   _____

5.   Bathsheba identified Solomon as the "who", his need for discipline as the "what" and now in verses 8 and 9, she explains the "why". Do we clarify the "who", "what" and "why" for our children, or do we expect them to figure it out for themselves?

_____

_____

_____

6.   Bathsheba had the confidence to help Solomon think about the gap between promise and performance. Do you think mothers today have the confidence to do this for their children?

_____

_____

_____

7.   Have you prayed about your child's promise? Does your child's performance indicate the promise will be fulfilled? How are you helping the process?

_____

_____

_____

8.   When Bathsheba tells Solomon about his "why", she does it in the form of a declaration. Have you made any declarations about your children? What are those declarations?

_____

_____

_____

9. We're all familiar with the scripture Luke 12:48, *"For unto whomsoever much is given, of him shall be much required."* Do we believe it? Do your children know (and understand) what they have been given?

_____

_____

_____

10. Was Bathsheba being unreasonable in asking Solomon to focus his considerable energies to help those less fortunate? Do we ask this of our own children, or would we rather they get a good job and make a bunch of money? How can we help our children calculate the cost of their choices?

CHAPTER 8

_____

_____

_____

"*Behind Every Great Man There's a Great Woman*"

W e all probably have heard this axiom a great many times. We may have even said it ourselves; possibly mumbled it under our breath when reading about some incredibly successful, allegedly "self-made" man and rolling our eyes over the afterthought-masquerading-as-footnote mention of his wife. But whether mentioned in a headline or a footnote, the truth remains, "Behind every great man there's a great woman". What is interesting to me is the fact that this statement is also used in reference to the role of a mother in the shaping of a great man, yet that reference doesn't seem to invite our collective ire, at least not to the same degree. When we examine the life of Jesus we see the critical role of his mother Mary evidenced from before the moment of His immaculate conception through the moment of His crucifixion. While many of His disciples were understandably too afraid to acknowledge Jesus at the moments of His physical death, His mother remained vigilant as recounted in John 19:25. *"Now there stood by the cross of Jesus his mother, and his mother's sister, Mary the wife of Cleophas, and Mary Magdalene."*

Yet, even before the birth of Jesus, we see ancient writings that speak to the love, regard and great expectations of many mothers. In the <u>Tirukkural:The Book of Wisdom</u>, an ancient Hindu text on virtue, wealth and love, we see a similar sentiment expressed. "When a mother hears her son heralded a good and learned man, her joy exceeds that of his joyous birth." <u>The Tirukkural</u>, the work of the poet and Hindu saint Tiru Valluvar, considered the greatest classic of the Tamil language, is composed of two parts, "Tiru" meaning sacred and beautiful, and "Kural" meaning concise. This description of a mother's literal pride and joy is a perfect example of this composition as it is both beautiful and concise.

I wonder why this awareness of the impact of a mother on the development of a great man, as seen in many biblical examples, such as Hannah and her son Samuel, is so comfortably acknowledged while the impact of a wife is not. This is particularly confusing given the fact that the positive impact of a mother can only be enhanced by her principle and primary role as a wife. Of course it must be noted that this biblically-mandated prioritization of a woman's relationship to her husband and her son is not always present. To some extent that lack of prioritization is inevitable in the wake of the growing incidence of births outside of marriage. What is more surprising and equally disturbing are the instances in which a woman elevates her relationship with her son ahead of the relationship she shares with her husband. That "re-ordering" is not new as illustrated in the biblical story of Rebekah's planned deceit of her husband, Isaac, detailed in Genesis 27.

While Isaac and Rebekah had twin sons: Esau the eldest, and Jacob the youngest; Isaac loved Esau and Rebekah loved Jacob. Genesis 25:28. Of course we see the common problem of favoritism right there; but that's another story. My point here is that Rebekah initiated a conspiracy with her favored son, Jacob, to deceive her husband, Isaac, and cheat her eldest son, Esau, out of his blessing. Beyond the problem of a lack of equity of love parents owe to all their children, Rebekah's lack of loyalty to her husband was the foundational problem that worsened that inequity. Nevertheless, Rebekah's role in Jacob's development as an unquestionably great man cannot be negated. But you have to ask, what must Jacob have thought of his mother as time went by and he worked through his reconciliation with Esau?!

And yet, as mothers, we all know how tempting it can be to pull our children into conspiracies against our husbands, their fathers. And spare me the look of shock and surprise. Have you never said "Don't tell your Daddy about this."? Well I have, and even though it was just about giving them waffles with ice cream for breakfast or staying at the beach all day eating nothing but hot dogs & grapes, it was still wrong. And I'm certain there were possible conspiracies on the other end. Who knows what went on during those Father-Son fishing trips and week-end camp outs? So, okay "all have sinned", one way or another, but we need to be mindful not to allow the love we feel as parents dominate the love we feel as spouses. In the context of this study then we are left to ponder the question of whether Bathsheba's impact on her son, Solomon, would have been not only as significant, but as healthy had not she first been a healthy and loyal force in the life of her husband David, Solomon's father.

Essentially then it appears (at least to me) that whether one is refer-
encing a son or a husband, the statement remains accurate. "Behind
every great man there is a great woman". While this truth may not
be convenient, comfortable or politically correct, it is neither oppressive of women nor demeaning to men; quite the contrary, the
axiom fits what we know of God's original plan. But I'm getting
ahead of myself. Let's start with the Bible, the Word of God as we
know it. That's one of the often-overlooked benefits of being a Bible-
believing, tongue-talking, "Jesus Only" kind of Christian, there's always an ultimate source to search, namely the Bible. From there we
can agree or disagree on interpretations and applications but we will
at least have some collective and constructive context in which to
explore this age-old discourse on the placement and price of women
relative to men.

Proverbs 31:10-12 *"Who can find a virtuous woman? for her price is far
above rubies. The heart of her husband doth safely trust in her, so that he
shall have no need of spoil. She will do him good and not evil all the days of
her life."*

We began this study of Proverbs 31, not at the typical point of introduction, the middle part, the part that encompasses the dream of
many men, you know, the fantasy woman who seemingly never sleeps,
never complains, never thinks of herself and never asks anyone else to
do so either. When this woman says "Don't get me anything for (fill-
in-the-blank)" she means it. In fact, her most consistent comment is
"Oh, don't worry about me". This is more than godly humility or
self-effacement (the act of keeping oneself in the background for the
sake of humility). This type of behavior acts as pretense of humility
and selflessness and whatever else it may be it is not a manifestation
of the love of self that God mandates. Yet, sadly, such ungodly mental
illness masquerading as altruism appears to be at the heart of much of

the widespread appeal of that glorious yet fictitious "virtuous woman". This is not to say the idea of a truly virtuous woman is an illusion as Proverbs 31 clearly validates her existence. But the virtuous woman, often cited out of biblical context, and used as an indictment of other women, is not only fictitious, but ungodly in her psychological martyrdom that borders on masochism. And before you go off, let me explain my position on this. A martyr is one who enjoys and seeks attention and sympathy by pretending or exaggerating pain, suffering or deprivation and a masochist is one who enjoys and in fact seeks gratification from deprivation or degradation whether self-inflicted or imposed by others. How could either of these concepts mesh with the mandates of God?

Galatians 5:14 states, *"For all the law is fulfilled in one word, even in this; Thou shalt love thy neighbour as thyself"*. Here we see the standard set forth by God, we must love ourselves so that we know how to love our neighbors. Clearly we are not to become so selfish, so self-interested or so self-absorbed that we cannot love others. But neither are we to become so fixated on the needs and desires of others that we lose ourselves and our responsibilities to self-development in the process. We are not to seek pleasure from self- denial or attention from deprivation. Rather, we are to discipline ourselves so we can move beyond our personal comfort zone and love others as we continue to grow in the knowledge and love of ourselves.

A goodly portion of the challenge rests with the fact that love is not a passive concept existing exclusively in the mind, the intellect or the spirit. Love isn't just something you say, it's something you do. Or to paraphrase my mother; when one of us would say "I love you Mommy", her response was always the same, "then act like it!" While seemingly harsh at first blush, the point is valid. This is not a popular concept, but behavior that is contrary to your parent's expressed value or belief system does call the idea of love and certainly respect into question. This strident "then act like it!" is actually a modern reiteration of John 14:15 *"If ye love me, keep my commandments"*.

Across the annals of time, the description of love in its various manifestations has been examined by philosophers and psychoanalysts alike. Erich Fromm (1900-1980), an internationally recognized, German-born social psychologist, psychoanalyst and humanist philosopher articulated fascinating views of love in The Art of Loving, his most popular work, published in 1956. His earlier books, Escape From Freedom and later Man for Himself: An Inquiry into the Psychology of Ethics are tremendously challenging, intellectual inquiries into existentialism, alienation and overall angst. Yet his book on love has been the one that has captivated people across cultures and outside college classrooms because it encapsulates universal ideas around the topic of love. "Most people see the problem of love primarily as that of being loved rather than that of loving, of one's capacity to love."

Dr. Fromm saw love as a creative rather than emotional process and expressed the view that the idea of "falling in love" was proof of a failure of comprehension of the true nature of love and its critical components of care, responsibility, respect and knowledge. Based on his study of the Torah, (his paternal grandfather and two great grandfathers were rabbis and his mother's uncle was a noted Talmudic scholar) Fromm felt the story of Jonah and his initial refusal to save the people of Nineveh from the consequences of their sins, Jonah 1:2-3, was indicative of the lack of care and responsibility in most human relationships. And I've often wondered if Jonah's refusal might not also have been part of that sick gladness/fascination some folks feel when bad things happen to someone else, especially when it seems richly deserved. Erich Fromm was undoubtedly aware of the German term for such sentiment, *schadenfreude*, "satisfaction or pleasure felt at someone else's misfortune". Dictionary.com. Maybe Jonah's 3 day "time-out" in the belly of the whale was God's rejection of not just his disobedience but also his schadenfreude.

But when it comes to understanding love in all its various dimensions, there is no better source than the actual Bible and we have to examine all of it, including the New Testament for clear and complete instructions. This does not invalidate the Old Testament, the Torah or other Judaic teachings; quite the contrary. Jesus clarified that fact and the essential nature of Oneness, wholeness and unification in His commentary in Matthew 5: 17-18 *"Think not that I am come to destroy the law, or the prophets: I am not come to destroy, but to fulfil. For verily I say unto you, Till heaven and earth pass, one jot or one tittle shall in no wise pass from the law, till all be fulfilled"*. Jesus, with His dispensation of grace, articulates a broader and deeper understanding of love merged with mercy rather than justice across the New Testament writings. I Corinthians 13:1-13 articulates this idea of love and mercy beautifully and in detail.

"Though I speak with the tongues of men and of angels, and have not charity (love), I am become as sounding brass, or a tinkling cymbal. And though I have the gift of prophecy, and understand all mysteries, and all knowledge; and though I have all faith, so that I could remove mountains, and have not charity (love), I am nothing. And though I bestow all my goods to feed the poor, and though I give my body to be burned, and have not charity (love), it profiteth me nothing."

And here we see the actual elements of charity/love enumerated (I numbered them!):

1) *Charity (love) suffereth long,* and 2) *is kind;* 3) *charity (love) envieth not;* 4) *charity (love) vaunteth not itself,* 5) *is not puffed up,* 6) *Doth not behave itself unseemly,* 7) *seeketh not her own,* 8) *is not easily provoked,* 9) *thinketh no evil;* 10) *Rejoiceth not in iniquity,* but 11) *rejoiceth in the truth;* 12) *Beareth all things,* 13) *believeth all things,* 14) *hopeth all things,* 15) *endureth all things.* 16) *Charity (love) never faileth:"*

Next we see the compare and contrast components of the chapter:

"but whether there be prophecies, they shall fail; whether there be tongues, they shall cease; whether there be knowledge, it shall vanish away. For we know in part, and we prophesy in part. But when that which is perfect is come, then that which is in part shall be done away."

The chapter concludes with analysis:

"When I was a child, I spake as a child, I understood as a child, I thought as a child: but when I became a man, I put away childish things. For now we see through a glass, darkly; but then face to face: now I know in part; but then shall I know even as also I am known. And now abideth faith, hope, charity (love), these three; but the greatest of these is charity (love)."

Now, if like me, you are arithmetic phobic, were never a "math-a-lete" and never, ever got the bonus points on an Algebra 2 exam, you may not enjoy an enumerated or numbered list of anything-and that's okay. And if you weren't a literature or humanities whiz, the whole compare and contrast thing may not work for you either. But this biblical concept of love doesn't require academic excellence, skill or even aptitude for comprehension. This idea of perfected love defined is simplified concisely in 1 John 4:8 *"He that loveth not knoweth not God; for God is love."*

Essentially, Erich Fromm's secular view is accurate. Love at some point must be evidenced through behavior or it isn't love, it's merely empty sentiment ("a calculated appeal to feeling or emotion, especially one that is excessive and unreasoning"). And if love is an art ("the creation of beautiful or thought-provoking works"), then it requires conscious, constant and consistent mindfulness and effort. That's why it can feel meaningless when people sit in church and collectively, often mindlessly chant "I love you and God loves you too!" or "the Jesus in me loves the Jesus in you". How seriously can you take such sentimental pronouncements if moments earlier you passed several "chanters" in the hallway and they wouldn't even speak!? And, in a secular context, everyone who's ever witnessed romantic deception knows that *saying* you love somebody and *actually* loving them are two entirely different things. It's what makes the statement "I love you but I'm not *in love* with you" so confusingly absurd. Does that mean one is *in love* but there is no accompanying passion? If so, wouldn't it be more accurate to say "I *love* you but I don't *want* you"? And speaking of confusing, what does it mean when Christianity is used as civic religion that makes the requirement of love circumstantial, i.e., "This is a Christian nation" but in a "post 9-11 world", we are not required to love our enemies and turn the other cheek?

The problem with state sponsored, civic religion is that it offers a limited, watered down and sentimental version of Christ's teachings. Forget the perfecting, just the practice of Christianity can be challenging in this context. If you don't believe me, just look at a small portion of Christ's Sermon on the Mount recounted in Luke 6:27-36.

"But I say unto you which hear, love your enemies, do good to them which hate you, bless them that curse you, and pray for them which despitefully use you. And unto him that smiteth thee on the one cheek offer also the other; and him that taketh away thy cloak forbid not to take thy coat also. Give to every man that asketh of thee; and of him that taketh away thy goods ask them not again. And as ye would that men should do to you, do ye also to them likewise. For if ye love them which love you, what thank have ye? for sinners also love those that love them. And if ye do good to them which do good to you, what thank have ye? for sinners also do even the same. And if ye lend to them of whom ye hope to receive, what thank have ye? for sinners also lend to sinners, to receive as much again. But love ye your enemies, and do good, and lend, hoping for nothing again; and your reward shall be great, and ye shall

be the children of the Highest: for he is kind unto the unthankful and to the evil. Be ye therefore merciful, as your Father also is merciful."

Yeah, all of that's so easy none of us needs to practice! But I digress-again. The point is the secular world's lack of wisdom, understanding and insight about love is predictable because those who are worldly are by biblical definition in darkness. But we who are the light of the world should provide a point of illumination; for how much greater should the knowledge and awareness of love be within the body of Christ given our access to wisdom, light and discernment after the infilling of the Holy Ghost? Wisdom is readily available as stated in James 1:5 *"If any of you lack wisdom, let him ask of God, that giveth to all men liberally, and upbraideth not; and it shall be given him."* Furthermore, we are not just the salt of the earth; we are called to be the light of the world, the city on the hill which cannot be hid.

Matthew 5:13-14. *"Ye are the salt of the earth: but if the salt have lost his savour, wherewith shall it be salted? it is thenceforth good for nothing, but to be cast out, and to be trodden under foot of men. Ye are the light of the world. A city that is set on an hill cannot be hid."* When we say we love someone, all should be able to see and fully understand what that means. Whether it be agape, the selfless, God-like love of humanity; familial, the "brotherly" love one feels for family (nuclear, extended or fictitious "that's my play cousin"); or erotic, the sensual and passionate love-one of the chief hallmarks of a Godly marriage, our accompanying actions should support our claims. This requirement of evidentiary action is non-negotiable and should be as readily apparent as a uniform, tattoo, secret handshake, gang insignia or church clothes. As stated in John 13:35 *"By this shall all men know that ye are my disciples, if ye have love one to another"*.

We as women working to be healthy, strong and truly virtuous, must be obedient to the word of God and love ourselves-first; only then can we realistically expect to fulfill the requirement to manifest agape love to our neighbors, familial love to our families and the critical combination of agape, familial and erotic love to our husbands. Fundamentally the requirement to love is a bilateral rather than unilateral mandate; in other words, we are to extend love both to ourselves and to others. This requirement of self-love is one of the hallmarks of good mental health, which by the way is an unequivocal indicator and benefit of an active and effective prayer-life. We are not promised perfect physical health but we are promised perfect mental health as stated in Isaiah 26:3 *"Thou wilt keep him in perfect peace, whose mind is stayed on thee"*. The ill-fated fantasy involving the so-called virtuous woman as the perpetually self-effacing, martyr/masochist is clearly out of order with the biblical, bilateral mandate of love of self and love of others. So how did so many folks get it "twisted" into a dichotomous, either/or concept rather than the diunital, both/and ideal of God's design?

The problem may lie in the way in which we define and understand the words we use. We admire the concept of altruism and decry the growth of egoism, but often we do so based on a vague and somewhat amorphous understanding of those terms. Altruism and egoism frequently are used in opposition one to another. Altruism, "the principle or practice of unselfish concern for or devotion to the welfare of others" is the opposite of egoism, "the habit of valuing everything only in reference to one's personal interest". Not surprisingly, the secular world with its emphasis on fragmentation, asks us to choose one or the other, but that is another form of beguilement for neither alone is sufficient.

The focus on fragmentation so common in the post-modern, industrialized world typically leads to increased specialization. At first blush, increased specialization seems beneficial what with all its emphasis on subject matter expertise. But that view can evoke sharp rebuke when, as in the case of doctors and their prescriptions, there is a negative interaction between two different pharmaceutical products, recommended by two different medical specialists, with the purpose of treating a single organism-you or someone you love. But fragmentation doesn't just create obstacles to a holistic connection in medicine. We can see the challenges presented by blind loyalty to fragmentation in many of the professions and in its potential for adverse impact in our individual lives, our marriages, families, collective communities, churches and ultimately our country.

Modernity's relentless march toward the praise and embrace of fragmentation has led to a sharp uptick in complaints of alienation. The term alienation dates to the ruinous 14th century, a century in Europe marked by numerous famines, widespread malnutrition and corresponding waves of the Black Plague which took the lives of roughly 1/3 of the population of Southern Europe. Historians note the 14th century as one of intense economic and social depression and, you guessed it-alienation. Merriam-Webster.com defines alienation as "a withdrawing or separation of a person or a person's affections from an object or position of former attachment: estrangement from the values of one's society and family".

There is a more explicit social science definition and analysis offered in Britannica.com. "The state of feeling estranged or separated from one's milieu, work, products of work, or self... (1) powerlessness, the feeling that one's destiny is not under one's own control but is determined by external agents, fate, luck, or institutional arrangements, (2) meaninglessness, referring either to the lack of comprehensibility or consistent meaning in any domain of action (such as world affairs or interpersonal relations) or to a generalized sense of purposelessness in life, (3) normlessness, the lack of commitment to shared social conventions of behaviour (hence widespread deviance, distrust, unrestrained individual competition, and the like), (4) cultural estrangement, the sense of removal from established values in society..., (5) social isolation, the sense of loneliness or exclusion in social relations..., and (6) self-estrangement, ... the master theme, the understanding that in one way or another the individual is out of touch with himself."

An examination of some of its most familiar synonyms , i.e., "insanity; lunacy; madness; aberration; mania; delirium; frenzy; dementia; monomania (an obsession with a single thought or idea)" further clarifies the long term implications of alienation. Yet when we think about these terms, alienation and fragmentation, I'm not at all sure we see the connection. At its surface the trickery of fragmentation rests rather smoothly on the comfortable idea that each of us is independently responsible for our own happiness, that we must each find our own path and be able to say unequivocally, like Frank Sinatra "I Did It Myyyyyyyy Way!"

As U.S. citizens we are particularly susceptible to this kind of rugged individuality as it is encrypted into our political DNA. Thomas Jefferson, one of the founding fathers, and the third President of the United States, expanded on the utilitarian writings of the English philosopher John Locke when he helped draft the famous second section of the Declaration of Independence. "We hold these Truths to be self-evident, that all Men are created equal, that they are endowed by their Creator with certain unalienable Rights that among these are Life, Liberty *and the pursuit of Happiness.*" (Emphasis mine). As an aside, we must note that the Founding Fathers struggled with their own fragmentation issue of cognitive dissonance (a state of psychological conflict or anxiety resulting from a contradiction between a person's simultaneously held beliefs or attitudes). Specifically, the belief that all men are created equal cannot be reconciled with the practice of slavery actively engaged in by Thomas Jefferson and his peers. But I digress; let's return to the principle point of happiness.

The idea of the pursuit, the active search for happiness, blends nicely with Mr. Sinatra's declaration-and we know how tempting that is! But since I'm not certain happiness is a thing that can be "caught", the idea of its pursuit is a deeply flawed trick akin to the idea of "falling in love". And the punch line of this cruel joke? The fog surrounding the futility of self-gratification doesn't clear until many of the temporal benefits from doing it God's way have been squandered. The intensity of the current, global recession is providing countless heart-breaking illustrations of this fact. There are a great many people who sacrificed their marriages, their children, in fact their entire families on the altars of their careers. Then after 29 years, 11 months and 29 days of service, i.e., mere minutes from retirement, they watch in dismay as their entire division, organization or even industry is dissolved. All that's left are the bitter ashes of regret.

Similar imagery is present in that sad, awkward moment when you run into someone you've known since you were both "just a sparkle in your Daddy's eye", maybe someone who grew up with you, as they say, "in church", but they stepped outside the ark of safety and stayed just a tad too long. Folks who are the embodiment of the chorus from the Brewer and Shipley 1970's hit "One toke over the line sweet Jesus, One toke over the line." Or my mother's converse sentiment articulated in the song "It Pays to Serve Jesus". Those who either don't know or don't believe, or who think they have plenty of time, ala St. Augustine's "Give me chastity and continence, but not yet", those who think there's virtue in saying "I did it my way!"; have been, to coin a phrase, "tricked, hoodwinked and bamboozled". All I can say is "keep having them birthdays!" After they've squandered years (dare I say decades?) "finding" themselves, many people often are surprised to find they have been on the proverbial "slippery slope". Sadly, that slide too frequently ends literally at the end, after many friends and family members have tired of waiting; waiting for the realization, waiting for the recognition, waiting for the understanding of the futility of self-gratification. At the end of the destructive slide one is left with things, identities and acknowledgements that do not and in fact cannot satisfy. This is not a risk that emerged in the midst of modernity. Isaiah 55:2 speaks to this human tendency, *"Wherefore do ye spend money for that which is not bread? and your labour for that which satisfieth not?"*. When you add the often attendant loss of health and beauty-well all you can say is the inarticulate "Eeeww".

Now don't get smug and condescending- I'm not the only shallow one! I dare say we've all had that scary moment of encounter with someone in our same age cohort who looks so bad that we run to the closest mirror to check our own face as soon as they walk away! And that's hardly a surprise given what we know about scriptural warnings such as Luke 12:2-3, *"For there is nothing covered that shall not be revealed; neither hid, that shall not be known. Therefore whatsoever ye have spoken in darkness shall be heard in the light; and that which ye have spoken in the ear in closets shall be proclaimed upon the housetops"*. So to correct the current slate of skin care commercials, it is NOT free radicals that age our skin-it's the way we live. The current vernacular admonition, "You need to slow your roll-you doin' too much", is a variation of the old school wisdom that you can't burn a candle at both ends.

But back to the loftier idea of the virtuous woman; essentially we are left with the age old dilemma of humanity, the question Moses asked the children of Israel in Exodus 32:26 *"Who is on the Lord's side?"* That's the biblical compare and contrast to Mr. Sinatra's commitment to self-interest. God calls us not to fragmentation but to Holinesss. The truth of the lyrics in that old hymn "He Satisfies," lies not in satisfaction through fragmentation, but rather through completeness, through the Oneness of the Godhead and all creation, including the human family. With Jesus as our ultimate example, it follows that we must reject fragmentation in favor of Oneness, wholeness and completeness. There is no need to choose either altruism or egoism. We need not choose between the love of self or the love of others. Within the universe of Christianity, before we even get to the subset of virtuous women, we are called to love ourselves as the baseline for the love of our neighbors. This distinction of virtuous women as a subset of the universe of Christians is not an example of fragmentation, but rather one of order. So back to the examination of the truly virtuous woman defined and described in Proverbs 31.

The amazing attributes of the virtuous woman aren't revealed until midway through the chapter. And since our class has tried to be ever mindful of the admonition to behave "in decency and in order," we began our analysis at the beginning of the chapter with a clarification of both identity and relationship of the woman so defined.

Proverbs 31: 1, 2 *"The words of king Lemuel, the prophecy that his mother taught him. What, my son? and what, the son of my womb? and what, the son of my vows?"* The words of love this woman, Bathsheba, spoke to her son, Solomon, were considered by him to be worthy of actual notation-the man wrote them down- right there Bathsheba captured my attention! In the 3rd thru the 6th verses she explains the need for discipline in issues as personal as sex and alcohol, and again-wonder of wonder, miracles of miracles, her grown son listened to her. By the 7th verse Bathsheba has moved from her assessment and analysis of Solomon's personal habits, proclivities and possibly inherited weaknesses (remember, she knew firsthand the weaknesses of Solomon's father David) to an assertion of his duties and responsibilities.

I know of no scriptural indication that Bathsheba knew beyond a certainty that her son's impact would stretch across countries, cultures, religions and time; I am not aware of any prophesy presented by Nathan concerning Solomon's future fame, but Bathsheba knew enough about her son's "here and now" to give him what was essentially a "Mordecai word". Remember how Esther's uncle Mordecai cautioned her about the implications of her responsibilities, *"who knoweth whether thou art come to the kingdom for such a time as this?"* Esther 4:14. Bathsheba speaks to Solomon about his responsibility in much the same way Mordecai spoke to Esther when she admonishes him to *"open his mouth for the poor"* in verses 8 and 9. Bathsheba knows Solomon's wisdom and eloquence may not be the only reasons for his existence, for what the French call one's "raison d'etre", but she is certain they form a critical portion of it. She brooks no possibility of any lame, late, after the fact and all too common excuses like "If I'd known then what I know now". As we often say in church, "the announcements have been read into your hearing-govern yourselves accordingly".

In other words, it is seldom the case of a lack of knowledge but rather a lack of discipline in the wise use of that knowledge that derails us. We know, we've been told and taught-repeatedly, but hearing and listening are as different as wisdom and understanding. To quote one of the most worldly of secular philosophers, Frederick Neitszche, our challenge is not a lack of knowledge, rather "we lack the will to execute". The great country singer George Jones expressed the same idea in his 1999 autobiographical hit *Choices*. The words of the chorus are heart-breaking, the first verse is just as painful, and the second verse evokes a theme of consequences so common it's legendary. Even if you're not a country music fan (like me) you should definitely check it out!

It's very tempting to heed the request of stubborn, hard-headed people and just turn away and let them reap their just desserts. But just as Jesus saved a space for us-while we were yet hard-headed-we must be willing to work earnestly to bring others, especially our children, along even when they are initially unwilling; that is the manifestation of love. Isn't that at least part of the lesson of Jonah? We, like Bathsheba, must continue to pray with, speak with, and, when necessary, admonish our children, even after they become adults. Sure, our comments may not be welcome, but that doesn't mean they won't be appreciated–eventually. We have to persevere despite the predictably less than favorable response; or run the risk of Eli's fate described in I Samuel 3:13 *"For I have told him that I will judge his house for ever for the iniquity which he knoweth; because his sons made themselves vile, and he restrained them not."* Eli loved his sons so much he resisted the need to restrain them; he didn't want to hear their smug justifications or risk their angry rejoinders. Many modern parents share Eli's resistance to their ultimate chagrin. We may love them dearly but everything our kids do is not cute! Our children may outgrow "time out", spankings or being grounded; but they are never too old for a word of correction. Chastisement is an act of love, one that is non-negotiable with God. Hebrews 12:6-8 *"For whom the Lord loveth he chasteneth, and scourgeth every son whom he receiveth. If ye endure chastening, God dealeth with you as with sons; for what son is he whom the father chasteneth not? But if ye be without chastisement, whereof all are partakers, then are ye bastards, and not sons."*

Interestingly, Bathsheba receives none of the expected negative responses from her adult son in response to her bold and direct incursion into his "personal business". (Maybe her conduct before him as a wife to his father earned his respect?) There are no frustratingly flippant dismissals, no angry assertions, no patronizing lectures on the importance of "boundaries" for healthy relationships, blah, blah, blah. Solomon, a gifted and renowned orator, doesn't launch into a lengthy soliloquy about how it's his life to live and his mistakes to make. Of course we are familiar enough with Solomon's history to know he didn't follow all his mother's admonitions–and yes, those "strange women" Bathsheba warned about contributed to his undoing. But Solomon did listen, he gave Bathsheba the respect and deference necessary for her to take the opportunity to engage him fully with her mother's heart.

How did Bathsheba create the space for such an encounter with Solomon? I think the answer to that question lies in the rest of Proverbs 31-the part that is usually the focus of attention of sermons and Bible studies, you know the part about the continually working woman. And what exactly is it about such an image that is so wonderfully captivating to some (men) and equally appalling to some (women)? But before we get into the whole nuts and bolts of women's comparative work ethic as articulated in an old English proverb, "A man may work from sun to sun, but woman's work is never done," let's examine the introduction of this segment of the chapter, because it is from there its name and fame emanate.

Proverbs 31:10-12 *"Who can find a virtuous woman? for her price is far above rubies. The heart of her husband doth safely trust in her, so that he shall have no need of spoil. She will do him good and not evil all the days of her life."*

This idea of the virtuous woman is introduced well into the chapter, yet it has become the hallmark of the entire piece. Why is that? Is it the idea of rarity, hinting at exclusivity? Is it the idea of the hunt, implicit when the verb "can" is used in conjunction with the verb "find"? Is the challenge of the find tied to luck or to knowledge? The knowledge gap could only go to where to look, because the comparable value is stated-it is above rubies.

An intriguing aspect of a precious stone as a comparison marker is its imperviousness to relativity. Rubies, like diamonds, emeralds and sapphires are literally deemed "precious" and have been across time and cultures even though they are stones, literally rocks. The preciousness of these stones is not subject to specific cultural aesthetics as is the case with many other aspects of beauty. For example, there may be universal acceptance of the John Keats' poetic line "A thing of beauty is a joy forever", but time and place, age and race and lots of other things can alter greatly the definition of what constitutes beauty. Yet across the annals of time, precious stones remain just that, precious, prized and highly valued. No matter the country, the culture or the century no one offered a ruby says "Rubies are so five minutes ago!". The fact that a virtuous woman is compared to a ruby, a precious stone, tells us something about her timeless and immutable beauty. There is nothing old fashioned, antiquated, worthless or weak about virtue because it remains precious. And just as stones are plentiful, yet some are precious, women are plentiful yet some are virtuous. That comparative analysis, while true, doesn't mean semi-precious stones or just plain rocks don't exist or possess inherent value and beauty.

Garnets, opals and topaz are no less beautiful because they are deemed semi-precious. A well-tended rock garden can be peaceful, a handful of skipping stones can be a ton of fun at the water's edge, a carefully selected stone in a slingshot can be an effective weapon and a boulder can be used to close the mouth of a tomb.

Stones have been valued in most cultures throughout time. The Republic of Zimbabwe, formerly the Republic of Rhodesia, is named for the stone ruins of Great Zimbabwe. Great Zimbabwe or "stone buildings" covers almost 1,800 acres in the continent of Africa. Built between the 11th and 14th centuries, Great Zimbabwe is so impressive many European and English colonizers in the 1800s did not believe ancient Africans were capable of such cunning workmanship (being black and everything–see how racial bias limits thought and imagination?!). Anyway, by all reports, these stone structures, much like the Pyramids in Egypt, the 100 stone temples at Angor Wat in Cambodia and the stone and earthen construction of the Great Wall of China, are enduring and utterly amazing. Many stone structures can be described as useful and beautiful–but they are not necessarily precious; because while beauty really is in the eye of the beholder, it is precisely because of its subjective status that it so dwells in the perception of the individual. In sharp contrast, that which is defined as precious must meet external requirements, for unlike beauty, "precious" is an objective description and definition.

Here's a simple example. My husband actually thinks I'm beautiful but if he presented that idea for confirmation to anyone else (other than my Daddy) the best he could hope for would be the broader statement, "She's a beautiful person."-and believe me, he wouldn't even get agreement on that that from a lot of folks! As sweet as it is that CMadison thinks I'm beautiful, the hard truth of the matter is it has no objective merit. On the other hand, if he takes my engagement ring in to be appraised, it's worth or value is objective; the diamond at its center is a precious stone. Different jewelers might disagree on the relative attractiveness of the setting but the value of the precious stone is based on definitive, objective standards, namely the carat, color, clarity and cut of the stone. In that same vein, there are tons of women and many are good, smart, hardworking and beautiful, but those attributes alone are not necessarily synonymous with the scriptural definition of virtue set forth in Proverbs 31.

Proverbs 31:10-12 *"Who can find a virtuous woman? for her price is far above rubies. The heart of her husband doth safely trust in her, so that he shall have no need of spoil. She will do him good and not evil all the days of her life."*

So we know a virtuous woman is an exceptional woman, one to be sought out amongst the throngs of women that comprise at least 50% of the earth's population. We also know such a woman is more valuable than a precious stone. Now let's begin an exploration of the qualities that identify such a woman. *"The heart of her husband doth safely trust in her…."* What exactly does that mean? Well some of the meaning can be derived from the rest of the sentence, *"…so that he shall have no need of spoil. She will do him good and not evil all the days of her life."* Some of the parallel translations of the Bible offer insight into these affirmations. Biblos.com's Lexicon offers helpful Hebrew translations of biblical texts and I used it in researching this scripture. "Labe", Hebrew for heart, also encompasses feelings, will and even the intellect so the statement *"The heart of her husband doth safely trust in her so that he shall have no need of spoil"* is expansive. The Hebrew version of *"doth safely trust in her so that he shall have no need of spoil"* is "batach chacer shalal" which translates (Batach) "be confident or sure-be bold, (make to) hope, (put, make to) trust, to lack"; (Chacer) "to lack, fail, want, lessen, make lower, want"; (Shalal) "booty or prey."

In other words, the husband of a virtuous woman will see his possessions, holdings, inheritance, earnings and assets appreciated, preserved and expanded rather than belittled, berated or squandered. And the resulting economic and psychological security will reduce the need for booty or spoil, a primary incentive for many high risk financial, criminal or military excursions. Simply stated, the virtuous woman takes what is available in her household and makes it work for her family. Such a woman is too busy creating satisfaction to keep tabs on what "The Jones" have so she doesn't worry herself or her husband in trying to keep up with them.

A review of this same scripture in translations other than the King James Version offer further clarification of the original Hebrew text. The New American Standard Bible reads "The heart of her husband trusts in her, And he will have no lack of gain". God's Word Translation states "Her husband trusts her with (all) his heart, and he does not lack anything good". A reading of The Bible in Basic English shows "The heart of her husband has faith in her, and he will have profit in full measure". The Darby Bible Translation states "The heart of her husband confideth in her, and he shall have no lack of spoil". Finally, Young's Literal Translation reads "The heart of her husband hath trusted in her. And spoil he lacketh not". Moving beyond translations, an examination of various biblical commentaries is also insightful. "He will not need to use any unlawful means to gain his living" <u>The Geneva Study Bible</u>. "He shall have no need to use indirect courses to get wealth" <u>Wesleys Notes</u>. "He relies on her prudence and skill...no need of spoil, especially that obtained by the risk of war" <u>Jamieson-Fausset-Brown Bible Commentary</u>.

Broad study coupled with serious analysis and reflection highlight the singularity of the virtuous woman. She is one in whom her husband can confide and upon whose prudence and skill he can rely. This is hardly the description of one who is oppressed or deemed to be "less than." Nor are these the attributes of one lacking in awareness, confidence or love of self. And best of all, wisdom, prudence, trustworthiness and the ability to maintain confidentiality are characteristics that only deepen and improve with age, unlike physical beauty. We are beginning to see why such a one is defined as precious; and why so many are confused by the adage, "Behind every great man is a great woman."

In 1985, Aretha Franklin and the British pop duo, the Eurythmics, recorded a hit single , "Sisters are Doing it For Themselves", and the lyrics highlight some points of conflict and confusion around this concept. Granted this is a great song, with a terrific beat (I'll give it a 85!) and obviously Aretha and the Eurythmics can sing their collective behinds off, but the lyrics convey a concept that is more fragmented than biblical. In and of itself that shouldn't be a problem because presumably we, of "like precious faith" do not take our lead or direction from the secular world. Sadly however, increasingly, we see secular thinking creeping, ever so quietly into the church. So we have to be vigilant and literally thoughtful about the ideas swirling around us. In listening to the lyrics of "Sisters are Doing It For Themselves" I realized I have heard disturbingly similar statements in church; and while not an exclusive source, I do think such views, along with the number of husbands and wives who appear to love their children more than each other, contribute to the number of dysfunctional families in church. God calls us to self-love and self-actualization with the caveat of 1 Corinthians 14:40, "*Let all things be done decently and in order.*" This admonition extends far beyond the Apostle Paul's determination about what should and shouldn't happen in church-and who can speak! This call for order is a preventative like a spring tonic because we know what happens in the absence of order-chaos. And, if we need decency and order in church, you know we need it in our homes.

When we have "our priorities in order" as my mother would say, it not only creates order, but ease. Simply put, we must first love God, then ourselves, then our husbands and then our children. Our children are derivative of the marital relationship, not primary to it. When the children are elevated above the marriage the family is out of order. It's worse than being "upside down" in a car loan-and you know how bad that is! So, when we become wives, our gifts and callings are to become part of the collective of Oneness we form with our husbands. If we as sisters are in fact "doing it for ourselves", we are out of order and on the slippery slope of fragmentation.

Ephesians 5:31-32 brilliantly illustrates the biblical opposition to fragmentation within marriage, and by extension family. "*For this cause shall a man leave his father and mother, and shall be joined unto his wife, and they two shall be one flesh. This is a great mystery:..*" In an age of reason and fragmentation, mysteries are problematic right up there with seeing "through a glass darkly". We seek reasoned and rational responses to all of life's challenges, but some of those challenges are mysterious and their resolution requires faith and obedience rather than reason. We are awash in a sea of information and technology and while I love the ocean, it can be dangerous, especially in a storm. The severity of the storm of opinions about the role of women, especially in the face of ever-increasing access and opportunities can be overwhelming, especially in a secular world. But in any storm over water, it is important to maintain sight of the buoy-that's the sign of safety. In my own life, no matter the degree of chaos, I try never to lose sight of the buoy that says "Paula's Best Interests" and I make sure that buoy is anchored in the word of God. Of course I have had many occasions of hard-headedness; that's why I can recognize and understand it in my sons. I've turned and tried to swim away-and almost drowned, choking on the words to that old hymn, "Not where I wish to go nor where I wish to stay, for whom am I that I should chose my way? The Lord shall choose for me, 'tis better far I know so let Him bid me go or stay".

As I have been told that I have (enormous) control issues, the concepts in that song are hard to swallow-but, unlike ingesting sea water, I've found these concepts won't kill you! But each time "I learned my lesson" in one storm, I didn't always transfer that knowledge to the next one. Yet, the fact of the matter is, we don't have separate, disconnected storms-we just think we do, just like I used to think there were separate, disconnected oceans. But here's another physical example of the magnificent Oneness of God; according to the U.S. Department of Commerce's National Oceanic and Atmospheric Administration, "there is only one global ocean". If you're as shocked as I was check out http://oceanservice.noaa.gov/facts/howmanyoceans.html.

There are geographically divided seas-the Atlantic, Pacific, Indian, Arctic and Southern (Antarctic)-but they are not separate bodies of water. Pictures taken from outer space confirm that these bodies of water are actually one continuous oceanic mass. Due to a host of scientific, geographic, historical and cultural reasons, boundaries have evolved over time, but the fact remains there are no fragments of seas or oceans on this planet-there is one ocean. Similarly, just as there is one ocean, there is one storm but with many variations, like the various boundaries between the singular oceanic mass. In each storm the same survival techniques apply. Through the thunder, lightning, howling winds and torrential rains we must stay anchored until our eyes can see the illumination of the buoy or lighthouse. In the challenge of being a godly wife and mother, Proverbs 31: 10-12 is at least part of what I see illuminated on the buoy. "*Who can find a virtuous woman? for her price is far above rubies. The heart of her husband doth safely trust in her, so that he shall have no need of spoil. She will do him good and not evil all the days of her life.*"

CHAPTER 8 QUESTIONS

1. What do you think about Proverbs 31: 10-12? Do you think it has it been used out of biblical context in an effort to control and oppress women?

   _____

   _____

   _____

2. Have you ever said, "Behind Every Great Man There's a Great Woman"? Do you really believe it? Is your reaction the same when it's a woman's son versus her husband who is deemed "great"?

   _____

   _____

   _____

3. How do you feel about the quotation from <u>Tirukkural:The Book of Wisdom</u> "When a mother hears her son heralded a good and learned man, her joy exceeds that of his joyous birth."

   _____

   _____

   _____

4. How is Galatians 5:14 *For all the law is fulfilled in one word, even in this; Thou shalt love thy neighbour as thyself.* used and often misinterpreted?

   _____

   _____

   _____

5. What do you think of Dr. Erich Fromm's assessment that "falling in love" is a fallacy that fails to comprehend the true nature and requirements of love?

_____

_____

_____

6. Do you think Jonah's initial refusal to go to Ninevah was an act of un-love?

_____

_____

_____

7. What challenges does 1 Corinthians:13's delineation of love present to us as powerful women of virtue? Are these expectations realistic in our dealings with our husbands? Are they easier to meet in dealing with our children?

_____

_____

_____

8. Do we in the U.S. use Christianity as "civic religion"? Are we serious about the challenges of practicing Jesus' mandate and example of mercy and forgiveness and reconciliation put forth in Luke 6:27–36? Did the events of 9/11 carve out an exception for us?

_____

_____

_____

9. Do you think Bathsheba loved her son Solomon more than her husband David? Do you think she respected her son more than her husband?

    _____

    _____

    _____

10. Can you sympathize with Rebekah's desire to provide the best for her son Jacob? How do you think she justified her actions against her son Esau and against her husband Isaac?

    _____

    _____

    _____

11. How do we guard against elevating our children above our husbands? Why should we; is it easier to love our children than our husbands?

    _____

    _____

    _____

12. How does Matthew 5:13-14's instruction to be the light and salt of the earth apply to us as women? What are the differences between lighting something and salting it?

    _____

    _____

    _____

13. What are some of the challenges of the three essential forms of love, agape, familial and erotic?

_____

_____

_____

14. Review Isaiah 26:3. Do you believe this promise of "perfect peace"?

_____

_____

_____

15. How do issues of fragmentation affect us as we strive to be powerful women of virtue?

_____

_____

_____

16. How does the definition of alienation relate to our current economic and political challenges?

_____

_____

_____

17. What challenges does the "pursuit of happiness" present to the body of Christ?

_____

_____

_____

18. What is the cautionary message in Isaiah 55:2's question? What are some of the impacts our disregard has caused?

    _____

    _____

    _____

19. What can we learn from the story of Eli in 1 Samuel 3:13?

    _____

    _____

    _____

20. Are you okay with the old English proverb, "Man may work from sun to sun but woman's work is never done"?

    _____

    _____

    _____

21. How is virtue, described as more valuable than rubies, different from beauty?

    _____

    _____

    _____

22. "…No need of spoil…" Do we create psychological and financial pressures for our husbands (and ourselves) when we can't be satisfied? Do we work to preserve and protect our family's collective assets? Do we consider them to be collective or is it "my money"?

    _____

    _____

    _____

23. The lyrics of "Sisters Are Doing It For Themselves" are rational and reasonable. How do you reconcile them with Ephesians 5:31–32?

   _____

   _____

   _____

24. What are the risks of drowning in this sea of information amid the storms of life? What do you think about the fact that there is just one oceanic mass?

   _____

   _____

   _____

25. How does the mandate to do everything in decency and in order apply to our lives as virtuous women?

   _____

   _____

   _____

CHAPTER 9

"My Family Is My Mission Field"

It can be a dirty job at times, but somebody has to do it.

Okay, we are finally approaching the most well-known segment of Proverbs 31. We have examined the advice and admonitions Bathsheba offered her son Solomon and we've conducted that examination from every available perspective. We explored Bathsheba's love for Solomon and her recognition of his beauty, his wisdom, and his wealth all in holistic conjunction with his lineage and his political and spiritual responsibility.

Throughout the process of examination and exploration, one comment and ensuing question continue to surface. The comment? Solomon has achieved the age of majority when Bathsheba initiates the conversation made famous in Proverbs 31. Simply stated, Solomon is already grown when Bathsheba begins commenting about his (very) personal life. She leaves nothing unsaid, no stone untouched, no subject is off-limits. Bathsheba states her views about wine, women, rule and responsibility with great and detailed specificity. Her views, while insightful, are somewhat predictable. What is not predictable and is in fact worthy of commentary and analysis is the fact that Solomon, an adult, a man, an individual in possession of beauty, wealth and power not only listens to his mother's discourse about life and his role in it, he is attentive, respectful and wise enough to record it. Now that begs the resulting question. How did Bathsheba create such a space of respect? And how did she have the boldness, the confidence to step into it?

Let's begin with a look at some of the descriptive elements of Solomon's life at the moment Bathsheba inserts her commentary. Solomon is *an adult, a man, an individual in possession of beauty, wealth and power;* each descriptor comes complete its own "boundary issues". Today, even in our current world of hard-won gender equity (at least in theory), it is often difficult for women to give a word of advice or correction to a child who has reached adulthood. And if that child is male, the challenge exists even if that boy/male child is not yet an adult. And what of beauty? Have we not seen instances where both the parent and child are in agreement that the child is too cute to be corrected, too precious to be punished, too darling to be disciplined? Wealth too can create mutually agreed upon barriers to correction. In an economic system of capitalism, often corrupted by conspicuous consumption, wealth frequently is confused with worth. Such a corruption of values can make it hard for a mother to provide a word of correction to a child whose pre-tax earnings are equal to or exceed her own. And of course this challenge is enlarged if the mother has laid the groundwork for the confusion in values through her relationship with the father. ("This is *my* money"; or "You don't make enough to tell me what to do!")

If beauty and money can be corrosive, then we would be wise to remember a secular admonition about power written by Lord Acton in an 1887 letter to Bishop Mandell Creighton: "Power tends to corrupt, and absolute power corrupts absolutely. Great men are almost always bad men". Essentially power, much like wealth, beauty, adulthood and gender contain boundary issues that can create barriers to correction; and it is the absence of correction that precedes stagnation and corruption.

Bathsheba was advising her son about power's myriad forms and dangers centuries before Lord Acton, the 19th century scholar on political liberty, wrote to Bishop Creighton, the Bishop of London, about the corrosive potential of unchecked political power. Bathsheba knew her son was destined for greatness and she was more than willing to utilize her position as his mother to facilitate his growth through reasoned analysis clothed in love and respect. What is especially amazing is the fact that Bathsheba provided this reasoned analysis to her adult son, not in the 21st century but in the midst of the Old Testament era of rigid paternalism. This required more than her willingness to step "outside the box"; Solomon had to be willing to let her step outside the box and he had to be willing to step out with her. How did that happen? How did Bathsheba create a space of exchange between herself and her son, a space that defied the social, political, cultural and religious norms of the times?

Perhaps Proverbs 31:13-27 highlights more than one woman's enormous work ethic. These efforts, more than the drudgery often dismissed as antiquated and oppressive may well be the wedge that created that critical space. Contrary to popular belief, the well-worn adage "God helps those who help themselves" is not biblical. Yet there is a scriptural requirement of energy and effort as evidence of faith. James 2:14-26 provides clarification that is brilliant in its illumination of this point.

"What doth it profit, my brethren, though a man say he hath faith, and have not works? Can faith save him? If a brother or sister be naked, and destitute of daily food, And one of you say unto them, Depart in peace, be ye warmed and filled; notwithstanding ye give them not those things which are needful to the body; What doth it profit? Even so faith, if it hath not works, is dead, being alone.

Yea, a man may say, Thou hast faith, and I have works: shew me thy faith without thy works, and I will shew thee my faith by my works. Faith without works is dead. Thou believest that there is one God; thou doest well: the devils also believe, and tremble. But wilt thou know, O vain man, that faith without works is dead? Was not Abraham our father justified by works, when he had offered Isaac his son upon the altar? Seest thou how faith wrought with his works, and by works was faith made perfect? And the scripture was fulfilled which saith, Abraham believed God, and it was imputed unto him for righteousness: and he was called the Friend of God.

Ye see then how that by works a man is justified, and not by faith only. Likewise also was not Rahab the harlot justified by works, when she had received the messengers,

and had sent them out another way? For as the body
without the spirit is dead, so faith without works is dead
also."

This New Testament scripture has a broad-based application similar to the equally illuminating Old Testament scripture in 1 Samuel
15:22-28 which highlights God's preference for obedience.

> *"And Samuel said, Hath the LORD as great delight*
> *in burnt offerings and sacrifices, as in obeying the voice of*
> *the LORD? Behold, to obey is better than sacrifice, and*
> *to hearken than the fat of rams. For rebellion is as the sin*
> *of witchcraft, and stubbornness is as iniquity and idolatry.*
> *Because thou hast rejected the word of the LORD, he*
> *hath also rejected thee from being king.*
>
> *And Saul said unto Samuel, I have sinned: for I have*
> *transgressed the commandment of the LORD, and thy*
> *words: because I feared the people, and obeyed their*
> *voice. Now therefore, I pray thee, pardon my sin, and*
> *turn again with me, that I may worship the LORD.*
> *And Samuel said unto Saul, I will not return with thee:*
> *for thou hast rejected the word of the LORD, and the*
> *LORD hath rejected thee from being king over Israel.*
>
> *And as Samuel turned about to go away, he laid hold*
> *upon the skirt of his mantle, and it rent. And Samuel*
> *said unto him, The LORD hath rent the kingdom of*
> *Israel from thee this day, and hath given it to a neighbor*
> *of thine, that is better than thou."*

So at the risk of gross over-simplification, I can deduce that (a) some work is required, (b) I don't always get to pick the work, and (c) a "do over" is not guaranteed with God. With those admittedly simplistic deductions in mind let's look further into Proverbs 31.

Proverbs 31:13-27 focuses squarely on the often demanding and sometimes tedious work of managing a healthy and prosperous household of peace and contentment. Such functional or "earthly" efforts can help create a space of daily worship in our homes in much the way praise and worship help usher us into service in church. Interestingly, the elements described in these verses match the elements of care and development in successful, secular organizations as well, specifically strategic planning, fiscal responsibility, and time management. Succinctly, in verses 13-27, Bathsheba transitions from the issues challenging men, including her son Solomon, to those challenging women, and she does it with the same clarity of focus used in the first 12 verses of Proverbs 31.

13. *"She seeketh wool, and flax, and worketh willingly with her hands."*
14. *"She is like the merchants' ships; she bringeth her food from afar."*
15. *"She riseth also while it is yet night, and giveth meat to her household, and a portion to her maidens."*
16. *"She considereth a field, and buyeth it: with the fruit of her hands she planteth a vineyard."*
17. *"She girdeth her loins with strength, and strengtheneth her arms."*
18. *"She perceiveth that her merchandise is good: her candle goeth not out by night."*
19. *"She layeth her hands to the spindle, and her hands hold the distaff."*
20. *"She stretcheth out her hand to the poor; yea, she reacheth forth her hands to the needy."*
21. *"She is not afraid of the snow for her household: for all her household are clothed with scarlet."*

22. *"She maketh herself coverings of tapestry; her clothing is silk and purple."*
23. *"Her husband is known in the gates, when he sitteth among the elders of the land."*
24. *"She maketh fine linen, and selleth it; and delivereth girdles unto the merchant."*
25. *"Strength and honour are her clothing; and she shall rejoice in time to come."*
26. *"She openeth her mouth with wisdom; and in her tongue is the law of kindness."*
27. *"She looketh well to the ways of her household, and eateth not the bread of idleness."*

Essentially, Bathsheba provides a descriptive context for virtue that is so broad-based as to be panoramic. She begins by equating virtue with excellence. And not just excellence as it is often used currently, as a popular buzz word. Allegedly, in today's popular culture, everybody is committed to excellence, just as everyone is a purported leader. But leadership, like excellence, is evidenced by action, not allegation. In her descriptor, Bathsheba makes this plain by detailing the evidence of excellence as virtue in the intersecting arenas of fiscal responsibility and economics; time management and strategic planning; and wisdom coupled with compassion, self-confidence and poise.

WOW! That sounds like a lot of work, precisely because it *is* a lot of work. But just as Bathsheba's advice to Solomon is best reviewed one verse at a time, the excellent work of the virtuous woman also benefits from an analytical review, a line upon line, precept upon precept, verse by verse analysis. In that vein, let's begin the process with a focus on function.

There are four distinct functional areas identified in this section of Proverbs 31:

(i)   *Domestic Arts*, highlighted in verses 13, 14, 15, 19, 22 and 27;

(ii)   *Economic Skills*, detailed in verses 16 and 24;

(iii) *Physical and Psychological Strength*, see verses 17, 18, 21 and 25; and

(iv) *Wisdom & Compassion*, described in verses 20, 23 and 26.

That being said, let's begin with the area least favored in today's secular and spiritual communities-Domestic Arts. An examination of verses 13, 14, 15, 19, 22, and 27 sheds a great deal of light on the mechanics of running an efficient household.

13.   *"She seeketh wool, and flax, and worketh willingly with her hands."*

14.   *"She is like the merchants' ships; she bringeth her food from afar."*

15.   *"She riseth also while it is yet night, and giveth meat to her household, and a portion to her maidens."*

19.   *"She layeth her hands to the spindle, and her hands hold the distaff."*

22.   *"She maketh herself coverings of tapestry; her clothing is silk and purple."*

27.   *"She looketh well to the ways of her household, and eateth not the bread of idleness."*

Starting with the first verse describing domestic arts, I reviewed more than fourteen translations of Proverbs 31:13, including The New International Version © 1984; The New Living Translation © 2007; The English Standard Version © 2001; The New American Standard Bible © 1995; God's Word Translation © 1995; The American King James Version; The American Standard Version; The Bible in Basic English; The Douay-Rheims Bible; The Darby Bible Translation; The English Revised Version; Webster's Bible Translation; The World

English Bible; Young's Literal Translation; and The Geneva Study Bible. Amazingly, at least four of the translations reviewed used "eager" or "delight" to clarify the "worketh willingly" aspect of this scripture. I find that amazing because I don't usually associate words like "eager" and "delight" with labor intensive work. Right off the bat then I can see a distinct difference between Bathsheba's approach to her domestic work and my own.

This is not to say that I'm lazy. I do a lot and it feels like I've been doing a lot forever-and I'm (only) 57 years old! I've been married since I was 21, a mom since I was 25 and a business owner since I was 32; and from all reports I do (reasonably) good work. However, and I think this is a critical point, I can't say my attitude about my work ever could be described with either of the adjectives "eager" or "delight".

Perhaps then it is not enough to do a lot of work for the work to be blessed; perhaps attitude is as crucial as effort. We know the axiom "attitude is everything" is true because it is confirmed elsewhere. 2 Corinthians 9: 7 states ,*"Every man according as he purposeth in his heart, so let him give; not grudgingly, or of necessity: for God loveth a cheerful giver"*. Of course we most often hear this admonishment with regard to tithes and offerings, but I don't think that is its single application. Often we tell our children about their "bad attitude", namely their seemingly incessant complaining and griping. But how much of that have they learned from us? We have to teach ourselves-and then our children, how to be happy in our work or whatever task is set before us.

Remember "*Whistle While You Work*" the song from the Walt Disney film, Snow White? My mother used to sing that song with us and as corny as it sounds, singing did make chore completion a lot easier!

And then of course there's the famous Charles Swindoll quotation about the significance of attitude. His assessment is correct for the simple reason that our attitude is the one thing we can control. We cannot control all that happens to us but we absolutely can control the totality of our responses to what happens. That's what attitude is all about-our reactions to our environment.

Okay, so now we know we must strive to bring an attitude of eagerness and delight to the critical work we do as virtuous women, if we truly want to release and utilize our power. But what exactly does this work entail?

Proverbs 31:14 states "*She is like the merchants' ships; she bringeth her food from afar*". What exactly does this mean? Wesley's Bible Commentator expounds as follows: "From afar-by the sale of her home-spun commodities she purchases the choicest goods which come from far countries". Sort of an ancient variation on the modern commercial "Choosey moms choose JIF". Seriously though, the virtuous woman is one who plans for her family including their meals, and while the occasional fast food treat is fun, it should not be an everyday event. But given the incredible demands we have on our time, how is it possible to plan meals, shop for food, put it away (which seems to take me almost as much time as the actual shopping!), cook it, serve it and clean up after it? Most of us today don't have the benefit of handmaidens, live-in domestics or even weekly Molly Maids so our husbands and certainly our children have to help; that's one answer.

The other answer lies in Proverbs 31:15. "*She riseth also while it is yet night, and giveth meat to her household, and a portion to her maidens.*" Hmmm… Verse 15 cites Proverbs 20:13 as a reference point, "*Do not love sleep, or you will become poor…*" as well as Romans 12:11 "*…not lagging behind in diligence, fervent in spirit, serving the Lord*". The New Living Translation states a more direct and pragmatic interpretation "She gets up before dawn to prepare breakfast for her household and plan the day's work for her servant girls". And again I say, hmmm… Okay, so maybe my actual challenge with the work load isn't just the management of my hours but the actual number of hours I'm up.

This functional aspect of the domestic arts component of Proverbs 31 continues in verse 19, "*She layeth her hands to the spindle, and her hands hold the distaff*". <u>The Bible in Basic English</u> interprets this as "She puts her hands to the cloth-working rod, and her fingers take the wheel". <u>The Douay-Rheims Bible</u> interprets the verse as "She puts her hand to strong things, and her fingers have taken hold of the spindle". And <u>Wesley's Notes</u> provides an interesting historical insight to this 19th verse. "She layeth - By her own example she provokes her servants to labour. And although in these latter and more delicate times, such mean employments are grown out of fashion among great persons, yet they were not so in former ages, neither in other countries, nor in this land; whence all women unmarried unto this day are called in the language of our law, Spinsters."

But this woman is not content to merely spin yarn. Proverbs 31:22: "*She maketh herself coverings of tapestry; her clothing is silk and purple.*" <u>God's Word Translation</u> states "She makes quilts for herself. Her clothes are [made of] linen and purple cloth". And <u>The Jamieson-Fausset-Brown Bible Commentary</u> defines coverings of tapestry as coverlets for beds. So this woman spins yarn, makes quilts for her family's beds and makes herself beautiful clothes! But as the forerunner of the maxim, "Pretty is as pretty does", this description of lovely clothes and fine linens references more than physical appearance; they are descriptors of holy living. Revelation 19:8 illustrates the point prophetically "*It was given to her to clothe herself in fine linen, bright and clean; for the fine linen is the righteous acts of the saints*".

This domestic arts section concludes with Proverbs 31:27. "*She looketh well to the ways of her household, and eateth not the bread of idleness.*" <u>God's</u>

<u>Word Translation</u> clarifies the verse as follows "She keeps a close eye on the conduct of her family, and she does not eat the bread of idleness"; as does <u>The Jamieson-Fausset-Brown Bible Commentary</u>, "she adds to her example a wise management of those under her control".

So what can we learn from these verses? Granted these verses are "just" about domestic skills, they don't address the significant issues of economic strength and fiscal stability. They don't speak directly to the critical components of physical and psychological strength and neither wisdom nor compassion are addressed directly. And yet these seemingly innocuous domestic skills are actually the foundation, the base upon which everything else stands. And if these cluster of verses, 13, 14, 15, 19, 22 and 27 form the foundation, then the cornerstone is in the opening phrase of verse 15, *"She riseth also while it is yet night,…"*

We all get 24 hours each and every day. Time and its constraints are some of the elements that unite all of us in the human family. So since there are exactly 24 hours- no more, no less-does it matter at which hour we decide to get up and get busy? Is there any real significance in starting the day (real) early "while it is yet night" as opposed to starting it at say, 7am or even mid-morning? "Early to bed, early to rise, makes a man healthy, wealthy and wise" Benjamin Franklin, 1706-1790; "the early bird catches the worm"; "strike while the iron is hot"; "make hay while the sun shines"; and even before the birth of Christ the lyric poet Quintus Horatius Flaccus (65 BC – 8 BC), more widely known as Horace, wrote in Odes Book I: "Dum loquimur, fugerit invida Aetas: carpe diem, quam minimum credula postero" which translates "While we're talking, envious time is fleeing: pluck the day, put no trust in the future". This willingness to seize the day (carpe diem) increases the likelihood of economic viability achieved through fiscal responsibility.

Proverbs 31: 16 and 24 speak to the issues of economics by illuminating the fiscal correlation between ambition, determination and drive. Ambition can be described as the desire for personal achievement; determination as the act of making a decision or establishing a purpose; and drive as the willingness to make it happen-"by any means necessary" to quote Malcolm X.

16.　*"She considereth a field, and buyeth it: with the fruit of her hands she planteth a vineyard."*

24.　*"She maketh fine linen, and selleth it; and delivereth girdles unto the merchant."*

Ambition is endemic. Lots of people have financial ambition, and I think that's especially true for women. We like "stuff" the acquisition of which requires bank, cake, duckets, paper, cash, or any of the myriad means of describing money. Who wouldn't like to have more money?! The desire for long-term economic security or even short–term financial success is one form of ambition that is widely held. So when I read *"she considereth a field"* I think, hmmm, don't we all: that's just a form of financial ambition. But the virtuous woman goes beyond ambition/desire; she doesn't just consider a field-*"she buyeth it"*-that's determination. And then *"she planteth a vineyard"*-that's drive. Verse 24 goes on to clarify this connection. *"She maketh fine linen"*-remember verse 19? *"She layeth her hands to the spindle, and her hands hold the distaff."* That's the process of making linen. But she doesn't just make stuff for creativity's sake-remember this woman may be creative, she may even be an artist, but she definitely is financially ambitious for her household. She's not just making this stuff to hoard it. She makes this linen *"and selleth it"* so some of her sales are direct. *"...And delivereth girdles unto the merchant"* so apparently some of the sales are consignment.

Remember "She works hard for the money" the line from the late Donna Summers' big hit? The virtuous woman described in Proverbs

31 works hard for everything! She takes her financial ambition and marries it to determination and drive. She doesn't just think about economic independence, she considers a field and then she buys it. She plants a vineyard, she makes linen and she sells her wares-she works hard for the money; and you can bet she's up early doing it! This sister is not the gold digger castigated by Kanye West and Jamie Fox, nor would she likely be interested in men whose lives are defined by entertainment. This is a serious sister, the kind of sister who would bring a level of seriousness to her choice of a mate. This idea of serious selection is particularly salient today when (Praise God!) we are no longer burdened with unilateral marital decisions made for us by our fathers, brothers or uncles. We need to take the idea of selection more seriously when we marry and mate; everyone is not worthy of reproduction-at least not at this moment in time. The virtuous woman knows and is consciously aware of that fact.

The third functional area in Proverbs 31 deals with physical and psychological strength in verses 17, 18, 21 and 25. Contrary to conventional wisdom, women are not weak. How could we be? scripturally women are derivative, Genesis 2:22 *"And the rib, which the LORD God had taken from man, made he a woman"*. As men were designed to be strong, so must women as their derivative be strong; otherwise, we could not be *"an help meet for him"*. Genesis 2:20. Proverbs 31 provides detailed descriptions of woman's strength.

Proverbs 31:17 states *"She girdeth her loins with strength, and strengtheneth her arms"*. <u>Clarke's Commentary on the Bible</u> clarifies this scripture in the following statement:"She takes care of her own health and strength, not only by means of useful labor, but by healthy exercise. She avoids what might enervate her body, or soften her mind - she is ever active, and girt ready for every necessary exercise. Her loins are firm, and her arms strong." <u>Keil and Delitzsch Biblical Commentary on the Old Testament</u> also addresses this issue. "Strength is as the girdle which she wraps around her body… Thus girded with strength, out of this fulness of strength she makes firm or steels her arms …The produce of the field and vineyard extend far beyond the necessity of her house; thus a great portion is brought to sale, and the gain thence arising stimulates the industry and the diligence of the unwearied woman."

We see clearly then that physical strength constitutes one of the variables of the virtuous woman. Yet this shouldn't be a surprise to us, because conventional wisdom notwithstanding, anyone who has seen a mother carrying a child fully half her size on her hip knows the idea of women as the weaker sex is a myth. And historically the myth of women's weakness has been disproven time and time again, and nowhere more painfully than in the lives of black women in the United States. Perhaps Sojourner Truth's famous speech, known as "Ain't I A Woman?" clarifies the illusion of weakness best. Sojourner Truth, born a slave in New York State, became a famous anti-slavery orator. She delivered her famous speech at the Women's Convention in Akron, Ohio on May 29, 1851. An original version of the speech was transcribed by a newspaper editor, Marius Robinson, but the speech became widely reported after Frances Dana Barker Gage published it 12 years later-with considerable literary license.

Most notably, Ms. Gage substituted the question "Ain't I a woman?" for Sojourner's actual inquiry "Can any man do more than that?" Gage also inserted Southern slave speech characteristics, presumably to make the speech more palatable to her reading audience. However, Sojourner was born and raised in New York and Dutch was her first language, so she had no traditional Southern slave dialect. Nevertheless the speech was and remains critical to the analysis of the role of black women in American society and it is especially helpful in dispelling the myth of women as weak.

Sojourner Truth:

"I want to say a few words about this matter. I am a woman's rights. I have as much muscle as any man, and can do as much work as any man. I have plowed and reaped and husked and chopped and mowed, and can any man do more than that? I have heard much about the sexes being equal. I can carry as much as any man, and can eat as much too, if I can get it. I am as strong as any man that is now. As for intellect, all I can say is, if a woman have a pint, and a man a quart – why can't she have her little pint full? You need not be afraid to give us our rights for fear we will take too much, – for we can't take more than our pint'll hold. The poor men seems to be all in confusion, and don't know what to do. Why children, if you have woman's rights, give it to her and you will feel better. You will have your own rights, and they won't be so much trouble. I can't read, but I can hear. I have heard the bible and have learned that Eve caused man to sin. Well, if woman upset the world, do give her a chance to set it right side up again. The Lady has spoken about Jesus, how he never spurned woman from him, and she was right. When Lazarus died, Mary and Martha came to him with faith and love and besought him to raise their brother. And Jesus wept and Lazarus came forth. And how came Jesus into the world? Through God who created him and the woman who bore him. Man, where was your part? But the women are coming up blessed be God and a few of the men are coming up with them. But man is in a tight place, the poor slave is on him, woman is coming on him, he is surely between a hawk and a buzzard."

We often hear disparaging comments about women working outside the home, and especially so-called "working mothers" but such negative commentary is neither scriptural as seen in Proverbs 31, nor historically accurate. And, in point of fact, all mothers are working mothers–it's just that some of us get paid for our work! While these comments about working women frequently are couched in protectionist language, they are often a cover for male dominance and control. As for the issue of comparable weakness, Sojourner Truth's question, "Can any man do more than that?' is rhetorical–the answer is "NO!"

Having dispensed with the issue of physical strength, let's move on to the equally critical elements of psychological strength. Verse 18 states *"She perceiveth that her merchandise is good: her candle goeth not out by night."* Merriam-Webster.com defines perceives as "to attain awareness or understanding" and "to become aware of through the senses". Essentially then, the virtuous woman knows her worth and the worth of her work; she needs no validation from others. This independent awareness of the self is foundational to sound psychological health. The thoughts that emerge from this self-confidence are critical as seen in Proverbs 23:7 *"As a man thinketh in his heart, so is he."* Confidence is vital if fear is to be forestalled. The virtuous woman is fearless, not because she is unaware of potential dangers, nor is she vainly unaware of her own limitations. She is able to beat back fear because of her knowledge of and confidence in God. 2 Timothy 1:7 *"For God hath not given us the spirit of fear; but of power, and of love, and of a sound mind."*

The virtuous woman described in Proverbs 31:21 acts as a forerunner of Timothy's oft-quoted words. Her confidence and preparedness stave off fear as eloquently stated in Proverbs 31:21, *"She is not afraid of the snow for her household: for all her household are clothed with scarlet."* It is important to note that this reference to scarlet is not a reflection on the virtuous woman's fashion forward thinking. She is not afraid of the snow for her household because she has prepared her household, physically and spiritually, for just such an occurrence. Storms and harsh weather, whether physical or spiritual, are not always predictable, but they are inevitable. Researching this scripture clarified for me that the virtuous woman's preparation, based upon her knowledge of the inevitability of storms, cold, snow, crisis, etc. extended beyond the physical. Gill's <u>Exposition of the Entire Bible</u> speaks to this duality of physical and spiritual preparedness in clarifying the use of the word "scarlet".

"for all her household are clothed with scarlet: the Vulgate Latin version renders it, "with double" (u), that is, with double garments; ... since the scarlet colour is no fence against cold, no more than any other, whereas double garments are; and which may be applied to the garment of justification, or the robe of Christ's righteousness, as one; and to the garment of sanctification, internal and external, as the other; the one, ... is an hiding place from the wind, and a covert from the storm; ... and the other is a screen from the malicious insinuations and reproaches of men... But had the word been designed to signify "double", it would have been in the "dual" number; as it is not, and is always used in this form for "scarlet"; ... which colour is an emblem of the blood of Christ, by which the church is justified, Romans 5:9; and all the household of faith, the whole family of Christ and household of God, are all justified by the same righteousness of Christ, consisting of his active and passive obedience, for the whole of which his crimson blood is put; it is a garment down to the feet, which covers all his people; they are all made righteous by the one obedience of Christ; they are all clothed in scarlet alike, all kings and priests unto God, all alike justified, and shall be glorified alike. The literal sense is, that if her household are clothed in scarlet in common; much more may it be thought that coarse and suitable garments would be provided for them, to protect them from the cold in winter (w)."

This is as good a time as any to redirect and refocus our attention on the New Testament admonition in 2 Timothy 2:15 "*Study to shew thyself approved unto God, a workman that needeth not to be ashamed, rightly dividing the word of truth.*" Granted this is not nearly as much fun-or as easy-as the more frequently quoted scripture, "*Make a joyful noise*"; but maybe we need to be both studious and noisy. Sela!

The virtuous woman prepares her household through her diligent physical activities and through constant intercessory prayer. Hence she has no reason to live in a state of perpetual fear and anxiety about future cold or storms. And this from a woman who did not have the reassurance of the resurrection or the Holy Ghost! How much more prepared, confident, fearless and psychologically strong should we be? Adding to her psychological strength is a sense of gladness. Proverbs 31:25: *"Strength and honour are her clothing; and she shall rejoice in time to come."* The various interpretations of this scripture clarify the meaning of the text. The New International Version (©1984) states "She is clothed with strength and dignity; she can laugh at the days to come." The New Living Translation (©2007) reads "She is clothed with strength and dignity, and she laughs without fear of the future." The English Standard Version (©2001) says "Strength and dignity are her clothing, and she laughs at the time to come." The New American Standard Bible (©1995) reports "Strength and dignity are her clothing, and she smiles at the future." And GOD'S WORD® Translation (©1995) says "She dresses with strength and nobility, and she smiles at the future." There's nothing like confidence and preparedness to evoke a sense of joy!

Having reviewed the first three functional areas, namely domestic arts, economic skills and physical and psychological strength, we are left with the final functional area, wisdom and compassion, detailed in Proverbs 31:20, 23, 26.

As much as the virtuous woman cares for her family, she realizes that she and they live in community with others. It is not enough to ensure only the care and comfort of her family. Part of what drives her industry is the realization of her affirmative duty to be aware of and whenever possible supply the needs of others. Proverbs 31:20 states, *"She stretcheth out her hand to the poor; yea, she reacheth forth her hands to the needy."* This is about much more than traditional alms or in current parlance, United Way drives, Thanksgiving soup kitchen volunteer opportunities or Christmas canned food collections. This references a kind of full-bodied compassion that stems from full consciousness, i.e., awareness of self and others. While self-awareness is indeed a critical first step on the path to sound mental health, the journey remains incomplete without a commensurate awareness of others. The virtuous woman is diligent in her aid, support and encouragement of others. She doesn't wait to be asked; she looks and sees what is needed, both in her own household and in the households of others. And when she supplies those needs, she is careful not to undermine the self-esteem of the beneficiaries. She does not need to be recognized so she doesn't need to publicize her "good works". She is indeed a cheerful (and quiet) giver, an embodiment of compassion.

Much has been written about compassion, its definition and manifestation. Thomas Merton, the famed Catholic theologian wrote "Compassion is the keen awareness of the interdependence of all things." The 1940s ground breaking developmental psychologist and Columbia University professor, Arthur Jersild, defined compassion as "the ultimate and most meaningful embodiment of emotional maturity. It is through compassion that a person achieves the highest peak and deepest reach in his or her search for self-fulfillment". Episcopalian priest and theologian Matthew Fox (not the actor!) said "Compassion is not sentiment but is making justice and doing works of mercy. Compassion is not a moral commandment but a flow and overflow of the fullest human and divine energies". And finally, the writings of the Dalai Lama state "The whole purpose of religion is to facilitate love and compassion, patience, tolerance, humility, forgiveness". How much more should we "of like precious faith", having received the revelation of the Oneness of the Godhead and the infilling of the Holy Ghost, embrace the call to universal compassion even as we care for our individual families!

I am convinced that much of our ability to embrace compassion is tied to our development of wisdom. Wisdom is not merely something that exists in our minds, it is not exclusively esoteric. To paraphrase the late, great, James Brown, the hardest working man in show business, in his mega-hit *The Big Payback*, "wisdom is a thing you gotta see!" There are few situations better designed to illuminate the wisdom of a virtuous woman than the community's assessment of her husband. This is tough, especially if you're a woman who married a man a few fries short of a Happy Meal. But, tough or not, the scripture is not wavering.

Proverbs 31:23 reads *"Her husband is known in the gates, when he sitteth among the elders of the land"*. I was very curious to read some of the writings and interpretations of this text. Barnes' Notes on the Bible states, "The industry of the wife leaves the husband free to take his place among the elders that sit in councils". Again we see the conflict between many current writers' and theologians' admonishments about women working, as here the work of the wife is essential for the freedom of the husband to "take his place". Clarke's Commentary on the Bible goes further in describing this co-dependency inherent in the phrase *her husband is known in the gates*. "She is a loving wife, and feels for the respectability and honor of her husband. He is an elder among his people, and he sits as a magistrate in the gate. He is respected not only on account of the neatness and cleanliness of his person and dress, but *because he is the husband of a woman who is justly held in universal esteem. And her complete management of household affairs gives him full leisure to devote himself to the civil interests of the community."* (Emphasis mine.)

How often, if ever, do we stop and think (seriously and prayerfully) about how our skills, talents, and deportment reflect upon our husbands and their reputations among their peers? And speaking of which, when was the last time anyone even used the word "deportment?!" As we strive to be powerful women of virtue, do we consider our deportment, conduct and behavior? I do not want to be a stumbling block to my husband. I don't want him filled with worry or anxiety about my ability to help create or manage our family's economic stability. Nor do I want him to cringe when my name comes up in public. It's easy to believe that the cringe factor is only an issue around clothing choices, but most of us have that covered. Do any of us really need to be told that leggings (or "jeggings") and a tee is not the best public fashion choice for grown women? And while we've all come close to the edge with a top a tad too low or a skirt a little too snug, we stop far short of straight out scandalous. But what of our demeanor, our deportment, are those elements even considered? Sadly, it's been a very long time since I've heard anyone speak of deportment, but the way in which we behave matters!

A virtuous woman, filled with wisdom, wishes to be a source of pride for her husband. Just as we women look at our sisters' marriages and draw sometimes unflattering conclusions about their husbands, we have to know that the brothers do the same thing. Do you want your husband to be pitied by the brethren? This is a particular area of weakness for me, especially in reference to the final verse dealing with wisdom and compassion. Proverbs 31:26, "*She openeth her mouth with wisdom; and in her tongue is the law of kindness.*"

Now, I think there are very few instances where my husband might be pitied for my lack of wisdom, but the whole kindness issue is another story. The Jamieson-Fausset-Brown Bible Commentary clarifies my challenge. "Her conversation is wise and gentle." Again, I could probably pass muster on the wise part, but gentle is not a word often used to describe my conversation or commentary. And I suspect I am not alone in this challenge. Barnes' Notes on the Bible elucidates further. "Law of kindness – The words which come from the lips of the true wife are as a law giving guidance and instruction to those that hear them; but the law is not proclaimed in its sterner aspects, but as one in which 'mercy tempers justice,' and love, the fulfilling of the law, is seen to be the source from which it springs."

<u>Clarke's Commentary on the Bible</u> also speaks to this dual requirement of wisdom and kindness. "She openeth her mouth with wisdom - ...now to the moral management of her family. 1. She is wise and intelligent; she has not neglected the cultivation of her mind. 2. She is amiable in her carriage, full of good nature, well-tempered, and conciliating in her manners and address. In her tongue is the law of kindness - This is the most distinguishing excellence of this woman. There are very few of those who are called managing women who are not lords over their husbands, tyrants over their servants, and insolent among their neighbors. But this woman, with all her eminence and excellence, was of a meek and quiet spirit. Blessed woman!" So here we see Clarke's analysis segmenting the issue further. First is the element of intellectual cultivation essential to effective household management. Second is the issue of "conciliatory manners" in general. Third is the issue of potential tyranny at home and abroad.

The first issue is fairly simple. For those of us with ambition, drive and determination, there is an inherent benefit to the cultivation of the mind. Quite simply, it's hard to make it, much less provide for your family and get ahead if you're stupid, ignorant or uninformed. The second issue can be more of a challenge for me. My manners might be viewed generally as conciliatory-as long as I get my way. But that clearly is not sufficient. And again, my hunch is that this is not my singular weakness and it may leach into the third issue, namely dogging out one's husband and kids. For me this third issue is tied to the self-interest element identified in the first issue. Specifically, I know of nothing beneficial that can be gained by disrespecting my husband-so I don't. Period. Even when I think (read that as "know") he's wrong. But the fact that I don't succumb to tyranny with my husband is not sufficient. We are called to kindness, conciliation and reconciliation with the entire household of faith. Now that whole household of faith part-that's hard. Because the fact is while agape love is real, I haven't found it to be nearly as persuasive as familial, paternal or erotic love. And all love requires work and sacrifice-in fact I'd go so far as to say that easy love is no love at all!

I love my husband to death. We got married in 1976 at the ripe old ages of 21 and 23 and when I think of how to truthfully encourage young newly-wed couples like our son Damon and his beautiful bride, Tanika, I reflect on Langston Hughes' famous poem, *Mother to Son* because surely life was not, is not and was never intended to be a "crystal stair".

Back in college, when I first read that poem, I thought it was about poverty, now I know it's about life and it certainly applies to marriage. But while it all "ain't been no crystal stair", I really do love Charles and the life we've built together. I love our sons, the men who once were the babies and then the little boys birthed and nurtured in that life together. And as an added blessing, I can truthfully say that I like them; I'd enjoy their company even if we weren't related. Because I love and like my husband and my sons, I can discipline myself to engage them not only with whatever wisdom God gives me, but with compassion as well. Maintaining that balance between wisdom and compassion is a much harder road to hoe with the entire household of faith. It's not that agape love isn't real or that I don't feel love for my brothers and sisters in Christ. It's just that compared to parental or even familial love, not to mention erotic love, agape love just doesn't generate the same degree of energy or heat. I know, it's a sin and a shame-but it's also the truth. And as a consequence of that truth, I have to work a lot harder to discipline myself in my dealings with the other "heirs and joint heirs with Jesus", those related to me spiritually, but not physically.

Of course, difficulty notwithstanding, the scriptural mandate in Proverbs 31:26 is constant, "*She openeth her mouth with wisdom; and in her tongue is the law of kindness*". Gill's Exposition of the Entire Bible explains the requirement as follows: "When she opens her mouth, for it is not always open, she expresses herself in a discreet and prudent manner; as well as speaks of things not foolish and trifling, but of moment and importance, and of usefulness to others: or 'concerning wisdom'...and in her tongue is the law of kindness; or 'the law of love'... grace and mercy; which is the law of Christ, Galatians 6:2; speaking kindly and tenderly to everyone, exhorting to acts of mercy and kindness, and doing them herself: or 'the doctrine of grace is in her tongue'." Okay I'll say it, that's not Paula; not even close!

The Keil and Delitzsch Biblical Commentary on the Old Testament assessment doesn't help me either; "The next verse presents one of the most beautiful features in the portrait: She openeth her mouth with wisdom, And amiable instruction is on her tongue... when she speaks, then it is wisdom pressing itself from her heart outward, by means of which she breaks the silence of her mouth ... Instruction which bears on itself the stamp of such amiability, and is also gracious, i.e., awakening love, because going forth from love...equals pleasing instructions,...- such instruction she carries, as house-mother (Proverbs 1:8), in her mouth...it denotes love showing itself in kindness and gracefulness,...Such graceful instruction she communicates now to this and now to that member of her household, for nothing that goes on in her house escapes her observation."

The Geneva Study Bible conveys the same idea, just more condensed, "Her tongue is a book by which one might learn many good things: for she delights to talk of the word of God". And finally Wesley's Notes interprets this verse as "She is neither sullenly silent, nor full

of impertinent talk, but speaks discreetly and piously, as occasion offers. In her tongue - Her speeches are guided by wisdom and grace,
and not by inordinate passions. And this practice is called a law in her
tongue, because it is constant and customary, and proceeds from an
inward and powerful principle of true wisdom".

Bottom line? The domestic work, even when done with eagerness
and delight is not sufficient in and of itself. Neither economic nor
fiscal wizardry in household management, standing alone, will suf-
fice either. Strength of mind, spirit or flesh, while certainly helpful,
will not independently unleash the full power of the virtuous woman. Each are critical elements; but the catalyst, the thing that moves
those elements from dormancy to potency lies in Proverbs 31:26 "*She
openeth her mouth with wisdom; and in her tongue is the law of kindness*".
In simpler terms, even if my house is so clean both my mother and
my late mother-in-law would be impressed; even if I can consistently
stretch a dollar 100 fold; and even if I'm so strong I can gleefully ask
Sojourner's real question, "can any man do more than that?"; absent
wisdom and kindness-well it just isn't enough. This really isn't a surprise, because we already know Proverbs 18:21 "*Death and life [are] in
the power of the tongue: and they that love it shall eat the fruit thereof*". This
is more than an affirmation of the good things that can come from
our positive speech. It is also a warning and an admonition about the
impact of all our speech-the thoughtless, the cruel and the vicious.

We began this chapter by exploring how Bathsheba was able to capture the attention of her adult son, Solomon. We wondered how she
was able to create a space in his life, a space so filled with respect
that he was willing to both listen and record her words. As we come
to end of this chapter, I can't help but think that Bathsheba created
that space by the prudent use of her words throughout Solomon's
life. My hunch is Solomon did not grow up listening (or overhear-
ing) Bathsheba screaming at David ("I can do bad by myself!"), or

speaking harshly (even if truthfully) about him behind his back to other women (Girl, I'm just going through!). I doubt Solomon heard Bathsheba constantly berating or gossiping about David's other wives or other women in the palace ("She ain't all that!"). It seems highly unlikely that Bathsheba spoke cruelly or viciously to Solomon ("Boy, you better sit down before I knock you down!"). Bathsheba must have exercised enormous discipline in all aspects of her life and part of her reward was the favor of her husband and the respect of her son.

CHAPTER 9 QUESTIONS

1. How might our behavior indicate we think of our families as our "mission fields"?

    _____

    _____

    _____

2. Does it seem as though other ministries are more significant or "sexier" than the ministries of our families?

    _____

    _____

    _____

3. How likely are we to follow Bathsheba's example and respectfully share our thoughts and concerns with our adult (or even adolescent) children despite their cries for "privacy"?

    _____

    _____

    _____

4. "God told me to take my hands off 'em." Is this a scripturally based mandate or is this a variation on "boundary issues"?

    _____

    _____

    _____

5. Do we wait too long to begin discussions about discipline with our children. Do grown children "owe" their parents any consideration re: unsolicited advice?

    _____

    _____

    _____

6. How does James 2:14 *"What doth it profit, my brethren, though a man say he hath faith, and have not works"* relate to our power as women of virtue in our homes? Can we have faith in the vitality and success of our family if we are not actively working to achieve those things? What does familial vitality and success look like? Can such things happen by accident?

    _____

    _____

    _____

7. *"Behold, to obey is better than sacrifice, and to hearken than the fat of rams. For rebellion is as the sin of witchcraft, and stubbornness is as iniquity and idolatry."* When we cite this text from 1 Samuel 15:22-28 to our teenagers, do we consider how it might apply to our interactions with those who have authority in our lives. Is having authority "in" (used to indicate inclusion, location, or position) my life the same as having authority "over" (used to indicate authority, power, or jurisdiction) my life?

    _____

    _____

    _____

8. Bathsheba lays out a plan of excellence for her household in Proverbs 31. Discuss your thoughts on the following statement, "excellence like leadership is evidenced by action, not allegation".

   _____

   _____

   _____

9. How might the confusion between wealth and worth complicate relationships? How might it undermine marriages? Describe instances where it might undermine parent/child relationships. How can that potential confusion be defused through the application of Romans 2:11 *"For there is no respect of persons with God."*? Does this earliest form of "equal protection under the law" mean God made everybody "equal" or the same or rather that God will judge everyone equally without regard to wealth or status or beauty?

   _____

   _____

   _____

10. A famous quotation reads "Power tends to corrupt and absolute power corrupts absolutely. Great men are almost always bad men." Do you think this applies to women as well? How might we, as powerful women of virtue, be subject to corruption? How might we guard against corruption in ourselves and those we love?

    _____

    _____

    _____

11. *"...Behold, to obey is better than sacrifice, and to hearken than the fat of rams. For rebellion is as the sin of witchcraft, and stubbornness is as iniquity and idolatry..."* 1 Samuel 15: 22-23. Do either of these well-known verses apply to us as we balance our power with our virtue? How so?

_____

_____

_____

12. 2 Corinthians 9:7 says *"Every man according as he purposeth in his heart, so let him give; not grudgingly, or of necessity: for God loveth a cheerful giver."* Does this apply to anything other than tithing and offering? How can an eager or delighted attitude affect our ability to complete the seemingly endless tasks that confront us?

_____

_____

_____

13. Can a determination to embrace each day fully and positively help to create a space of worship, first in our minds and then in our homes? Is praise and worship as important personally and privately as it is corporately and publically? Can it make a difference in our lives long-term?

_____

_____

_____

14. Is strategic planning as critical for families as it is for corporations? If so, what are some ways we can bring elements of strategic planning into our homes, our lives and the lives of our loved ones?

_____

_____

_____

15. What do you think of the correlation between ambition, determination and drive derived from Proverbs 31: 16 and 24 detailed earlier in this chapter? Dictionary.com defines fiscal as "of or pertaining to financial matters in general" and economic as "pertaining to the production, distribution, and use of income, wealth, and commodities". Is it unusual to see Proverbs' virtuous woman described as one involved in both the fiscal and economic health of her family?

_____

_____

_____

16. Why do we often think of economics in "macro" concepts of governments and corporations when the Greek origin of the word is *oikonomia* which translates "management of a household" (oikos/house + nomos/ custom or law)? See Wikipedia.

_____

_____

_____

17. How strange is it to hear women described both as the weaker sex and as helpmeet? Do you think the frequent description of women as weak is intended for our protection

or our domination? How does the conventional concept of women as weak bear up under the scrutiny of Sojourner Truth's critical question "Can any man do more than that?" How does it compare with the description in Proverbs 31:17 *"She girdeth her loins with strength, and strengtheneth her arms."*?

---

18. Have you noticed the deluge of advertisements for depression medication–and supplemental medication "if your antidepressant isn't working"? Mental Health America reports 21 million Americans suffer from depression. Proverbs 31: 21 states *"She is not afraid of the snow for her household"*...and verse 25 says *"Strength and honour are her clothing; and she shall rejoice in time to come"*. Might the virtuous woman's attitude/ approach have a positive impact on her life experience? Should it be explored as a possible preventative to depression?

---

19. How would you describe compassion? What role does compassion play in virtue? Can a woman be truly virtuous without compassion? Does the considerable effort necessary to care for our families excuse us from the duty of compassionate care for others?

---

20. "*Her husband is known in the gates...*" Proverbs 31:23. Why do women need to concern themselves with the status or public image of their husbands? "*She openeth her mouth with wisdom; and in her tongue is the law of kindness.*" Proverbs 31:26. What are some of the reasons wisdom and the law of kindness are often missing from our conversations? How can we help each other do better?

   _____

   _____

   _____

CHAPTER 10

"Actually, She IS All That!"

"*Her children arise up, and call her blessed;
her husband also, and he praiseth her.
Many daughters have done virtuously,
but thou excellest them all. Favour is deceitful,
and beauty is vain: but a woman that feareth the
LORD, she shall be praised.
Give her of the fruit of her hands; and let her
own works praise her in the gates.*"

Work well done is its own reward. And eventually, in the right time, at the appropriate time, in the *"fullness of time,"* Galatians 4:4, work done well will be recognized. Now, of course right off the bat, we're stuck with this whole control and command challenge inherent in issues of time and perceptions of timeliness. It's not just that we want to be recognized and acknowledged for our good work, we want that recognition and acknowledgement to happen when we think it should happen. And what's wrong with that? Well nothing except that we don't actually have control of time or the capacity to determine timeliness, God does. That's why there's inherent truth in the axiom, "He may not come when you want Him, but He's always right on time!" That axiom is derivative from a cumulative reading of several scriptures. Psalms 27:14, *"Wait on the LORD: be of good courage, and he shall strengthen thine heart: wait, I say, on the LORD."* Yes, I know, this references David's discouragement upon returning from battle and finding his wife and children stolen-and having to face the wrath of his men. And I'm not discounting David's angst; but women, then and now, face our own angst and despair-and lack of immediate recognition and appreciation. We too, like David, must encourage ourselves in the Lord until we come into *our* kingdom. In the midst of the waiting, it really helps to be mindful and fully conscious of the process while waiting with patience and confidence.

I believe it is in the act of mindfulness and consciousness that transcendence occurs; the kind of transcendence that makes the whole thing possible. Isaiah 40:31, *"But they that wait upon the LORD shall renew [their] strength; they shall mount up with wings as eagles; they shall run, and not be weary; [and] they shall walk, and not faint."* The following secular definition of transcendence found in Dictionary.com, "exceeding or surpassing in degree or excellence; free from the limitations inherent in matter", illuminates the power of that scripture. In the midst of conscious, mindful, waiting, God allows us to be strengthened holistically in our resolve-spiritually, intellectually and physically. That resolve is what allowed me to tell my sons when they were teenagers, "I can pray longer than you can clown!" And isn't that better than killing 'em and making it look like an accident?! Working at becoming all that God wants for us as powerful women of virtue is not easy and it's not for the faint of heart, that's why we have to support one another with the reminder of 2 Corinthians 4: 8-9, *"We are troubled on every side, yet not distressed; we are perplexed, but not in despair; Persecuted, but not forsaken; cast down, but not destroyed"*.

Those troubling and perplexing times when we feel persecuted-those are not just occurrences of spiritual warfare in the world. Sometimes our biggest challenges are in our own churches, in our own homes, in our own families, in our own marriages. That's why we cannot afford to allow one another to feel distressed, destroyed, forsaken or in despair-there's too much at stake collectively.

We must press on no matter how annoying the real or perceived lack of appreciation feels. Those days when you plan and prepare a lovely dinner, set the table and then somebody says, "Oh, I ate on the way home" or "I'm not hungry right now" or they come to the table like a cloud of locust and consume in 3 minutes everything you spent hours preparing-Gird up your loins and Press on! Often it's not the big ferocious attacks by the enemy that wear us down, we're prepared for those. The hidden danger is in the steady drip, drip, drip, the slow erosion of energy and excitement that can occur in the day-to-day lives of women struggling to maintain our position of powerful virtue. The relentless cycle of cooking, cleaning, laundry-and when you break those tasks down into their component parts well, it's more than a notion.

Before you can start cooking, you have to plan the menus, make the shopping list, cut the coupons, clean out the refrigerator and the pantry, go to the market and then put the food away. Before you can start cleaning, you have to pick up & straighten up-*then* you can start sweeping, vacuuming, mopping, dusting, polishing and cleaning baseboards. And laundry? Before that first load goes in the machine, you've got to strip all the beds, collect the linens from the kitchen and the bathrooms and everything in the dirty clothes hampers and then separate them; and in between loads you have to fold, iron and put everything away. Now we as women may not have to perform each and every one of those tasks, but in most instances we at least have to supervise them. That's why Galatians 6:9, *"And let us not be weary in well doing: for in due season we shall reap, if we faint not."* is especially relevant to women working in the vineyard known as the home.

In our vineyards, in our gardens, we work-and we wait. We wait for germination and we wait for harvest, knowing that we cannot speed the process along. One of the best things about my physical garden, beside the fresh, organic, pesticide & e-coli free produce, is how it forces me to practice patience and to wait with confidence. James 5:7 speaks to this process of confident patience, *"Be patient therefore, brethren, unto the coming of the Lord. Behold, the husbandman waiteth for the precious fruit of the earth, and hath long patience for it, until he receive the early and latter rain"*.

Yet the question remains, what to do while we're waiting? Psalms 37:4 *"Delight thyself also in the LORD; and he shall give thee the desires of thine heart."* I think this admonition about delight pretty much excludes whining, complaining and pouting. I think it's hard to feel delighted *and* unappreciated at the same time; but it's not impossible. We just have to know the reward of recognition is coming. Our husbands and our children will rise up and call us blessed-that harvest is coming; as women, we just have to believe it and wait for it. Even in the world the concept of waiting patiently is linked to the concept of gender.

Remember "All I Gotta Do", Nikki Giovanni's poem, where she talks about sitting and waiting, somehow knowing that what she's waiting for will find her? Granted, we as powerful women of virtue don't have a lot of time to spend sitting per se, but the concept in this sister's poem still resonates for me. This idea of waiting with confidence that what is wanted, what is needed, in this instance recognition and appreciation, will appear is a practical element of faith.

But before you roll your eyes, I'm not just speaking about heavenly recognition and reward, which will undoubtedly be more than we can imagine. The recognition I'm speaking of exists in this current physical realm, and it is not exclusively spiritual; it is a reward that we will receive in the flesh. But don't take my word for it-let's see what the Book says, specifically Proverbs 31: 28-31, the final verses of this famous chapter about the virtuous woman.

28.   *"Her children arise up, and call her blessed; her husband also, and he praiseth her."*
29.   *"Many daughters have done virtuously, but thou excellest them all."*
30.   *"Favour is deceitful, and beauty is vain: but a woman that feareth the LORD, she shall be praised."*
31.   *"Give her of the fruit of her hands; and let her own works praise her in the gates."*

These are the last few verses of this chapter and I think they deserve as much attention and analysis as the first twenty-seven; so let's start with the promise of verse 28. *"Her children arise up, and call her blessed"*; this first parenthetical phrase alone is enough to cause us to shout and do the happy dance. There is no ambivalence here, no wishful thinking, if, but or maybe in this statement-which is pretty amazing when you think about it. Sometimes as mothers, especially as mothers of pre-teens, full blown adolescents and even young adults we wonder if our children will ever just "arise". Forget the rest of the promise, just the thought of them getting up-voluntarily, not fussing, not complaining, no lip, whoa, my head is spinning. But this scripture reads as a statement of fact, an unequivocal promise; the virtuous woman's children arise, get up *and* call her blessed.

Run over in your minds the things you called your own mother-in your secret teen thoughts of course, not out loud. Now gird up your loins and try to imagine what your own children have called you secretly and couple that with what they've called you to your face: mean, unfair, unreasonable, controlling, nosy, blah, blah, blah. In the review of all those names did you come across the word "blessed"? Yet that is the promise and that is part of what can help us persevere. Earlier in this very book I talked about the danger of quoting from non-existent scriptures, e.g., "God helps those who help themselves". Now, I'm going to do it-sort of-by combining two portions of scripture into a "verse" I've heard many times. Ecclesiastes 9:11 *"the race is not to the swift, nor the battle to the strong…"* and Matthew 2:13, *"…But he that shall endure unto the end, the same shall be saved."* I think there's a reason we so often hear this combination of Old and New Testament verses coupled as one.

This life is a race, but even the P.E. challenged among us know there are many different kinds of races. There are sprints, relays, cross-country and marathons-and each require different skill sets; sometimes the fastest sprinters are least equipped to excel in a long distance run. That is a good lesson to keep in mind in our race as Christians. How often have we seen folks so on fire for the Lord they singed everyone in sight with their judgmental condemnation but ultimately were unable to sustain their walk? In junior high school there were kids who'd stop me on the way to the cafeteria with the reminder, "Wednesday is our Fast Day Sister Paula". Of course that just made me mad, defiant *and* hungry. Behind their backs my sister and I used to call them "Super Saved/Junior Jesus" (Yeah, I know that was mean, but that was 1967; we're better now☺). What is much sadder than my 7th grade bad attitude is the fact that many of those folks could not sustain that sprinter's pace in life's cross-country marathon over shaky terrain. We have to pace ourselves if we plan to endure to the end. That doesn't mean we lower our standards, it means we have to take the distance runner's disciplined long view, especially as we run the marathon of life, marriage and parenting.

Maintaining the disciplined long view of a virtuous woman reveals the power of metamorphosis from ungrateful children into ones who arise and call you blessed. And that's just the first part of verse 28. The rest of the sentence reads *"her husband also, and he praiseth her"*. Hold onto your church hats ladies, *"her husband also..."* The grammatical construction of the sentence means the subject in the second segment of the sentence, *"her husband,"* is repeating the behavior of the subject in the first segment of the sentence, *"her children"*. Literally, her husband also arises and calls her blessed, just like her children. But the promise doesn't just continue, it expands because the husband of the virtuous woman doesn't just call her blessed, he praises her. We shouldn't be shocked by the expansion. No one should benefit more from the presence of a virtuous woman than her husband, not even her children.

We've talked about this particular challenge before, the sometimes difficult balance between being a good wife and being a good mother. A virtuous woman diligently guards her husband's position of pre-eminence in her heart. We love our children, but we can't forget that they are derivative of the relationship that led to their conception. This reality of derivation is challenging for most of us-regardless of the status of our relationship with the father(s) of our children- because so much of what we feel about our babies is separate and distinct from what we feel about their fathers.

For most mothers, part of the challenge of derivation lies in the fact that our babies seem so, well perfect, so small and fat and marvelously made with that irresistible baby smell. Loving them, cradling them, almost adoring them feels natural. And they need us (and can be shaped by us!) in ways that their fathers, whether they're our husbands, lovers or past boyfriends never could. For married mothers, the challenge of derivation may lie in trying to make time for our husbands in whom too often we see just the limitations of past and present performance, while caring for our babies in whom we see only the infinite possibilities of potential.

For widowed mothers, especially when the children are still minors, the challenge of derivation may be combined with the painful loss of not just a husband but a co-parent as well. For divorced mothers the challenge may also contain elements of disappointment, anger and possibly shame. And for single mothers or mothers who never married there may be the additional issue of community condemnation or judgment layered on top of everything else. Regardless of the unique challenges we each face, and we all do, to enjoy the fulfilled promises in Proverbs 31:28 we have to strive to function as virtuous women. And when we do, our children will arise and call us blessed and our husbands also will praise us.

One of the real difficulties in the application of these particular verses, in this particular chapter, to our current situations is the range of these present-day situations. While there is nothing new under the sun, this chapter does not appear to have been written from the perspective of an unmarried woman; yet that doesn't mean the Word has no application for all women. Virtue is not the exclusive province of the married. But for those of us who have observed husbands, our own or others, how rare is it to witness praise, even in the face of virtue. Might that lapse, that conspicuous absence of praise in the homes of our parents and grandparents play into the decline of marriage? I'm not talking about the staged and choreographed public performances so often played out and presented as praise for official occasions. Praise is defined in Dictionary.com as a noun, "the act of expressing approval or admiration; commendation; laudation" or a verb, "to express approval or admiration of; commend; extol". What is implied in these definitions is a degree of sincerity, and without that, praise is as "sounding brass or tinkling cymbals".

Remember the scene in the Tyler Perry movie "Diary of a Mad, Black Woman" when the husband, as part of his award acceptance speech, praises his wife for helping him and then later that same night physically throws her out of their home? That kind of hypocritical praise, while sadly common, is not the kind of praise referenced in verse 28.

Long before genuine, sincere praise can be spoken, it must first be understood in the heart; and that understanding will be evidenced in action. We all like to be recognized and acknowledged, but genuine and effective praise is best illuminated in the light of our actions. The Old Testament is replete with admonitions of praise, none more familiar than Psalms 150, *"Praise ye the LORD. Praise God in his sanctuary: praise him in the firmament of his power. Praise him for his mighty acts: praise him according to his excellent greatness. Praise him with the sound of the trumpet: praise him with the psaltery and harp. Praise him with the timbrel and dance: praise him with stringed instruments and organs. Praise him upon the loud cymbals: praise him upon the high sounding cymbals. Let everything that hath breath praise the LORD. Praise ye the LORD."*

But the New Testament expounds upon the true motivation of praise. John 14:15 reads *"If ye love me, keep my commandments."* God wants more than our words and songs of praise and even more than our bodies as a living sacrifice.

Chastity, charity, modesty, temperance, these are all wonderful virtues but they are not unique to the Christian experience and did not require His crucifixion and resurrection to be actualized in the human family. There are many people of many faiths as well as atheists and agnostics who adhere to principles and philosophies of chastity, charity, modesty and temperance. Jesus requires more than good works and the physical restraint of our flesh, He requires the far more difficult and daily, private task of control and restraint of our thoughts and our hearts. He requires the actualization of love through obedience. John 14:15 illustrates syntax construction that extends beyond grammar to programming because the "if-then" statement is a basic control-flow statement. It tells the program to execute a specific code *only if* a particular test evaluates to true, i.e., "*If ye love me, keep my commandments*". In this scripture the word "then" is implied by Saint John and inferred by the reader; in any event the "if-then" statement is simple, but it is not easy. Granted, it's easier than computer programming, but it isn't as easy as praise.

Now before you get your undies in a bunch, just reflect upon the fact that it is much easier to praise, i.e., to say you love Him, than it is to keep His commandments. The proof? Turn on almost any award show and listen to entertainers, whose carnal performances would shame the debauchery of a bacchanal, start with the standard "Giving honor to God…" That's the spiritual equivalent to the husband in the "Diary of a Mad, Black Woman" movie. Just as God doesn't want empty, insincere words of praise, neither do virtuous women. We don't need public pronouncements of adoration and lavish flower arrangements sent to our workplaces nearly as much as we need genuine and sincere praise evidenced by action in our homes.

It's difficult to acknowledge or appreciate praise, even purported spiritual praise accompanied by worship when the person giving the praise has been hurtful. It takes the transcendent power of God to move us past our own hurt and anger. As a woman, that's one reason I can understand Michal's dismissal of David's praise. Unlike most commentaries, coincidentally written by men, I focused on how David hurt Michal-the only one of his wives described in the scriptures as loving him. In fact the Jewish Study Bible notes that 1 Samuel

18:20 is the single recorded place in the Bible where a woman's love for a man is noted. *"And Michal Saul's daughter loved David: and they told Saul, and the thing pleased him."* Further in verses 28 and 29 of that same chapter we see yet another statement of not only Michal's love for David but also an indication of how her father King Saul felt about it. *"And Saul saw and knew that the LORD was with David, and that Michal Saul's daughter loved him. And Saul was yet the more afraid of David; and Saul became David's enemy continually."*

Michal loved David so much she helped him escape her father's wrath–and then lied about it! Perhaps in retaliation, but certainly not in love or concern, her father marries Michal off to another man, Paltiel; a man who actually loved her. But after Saul died, David returned and reclaimed Michal–not because he loved her but merely to strengthen his claim to the throne. And we wonder why she expressed disapproval, disbelief and even animus about the sincerity of his near-naked dance of praise? 2 Samuel 6:20 reads in part *"And Michal the daughter of Saul came out to meet David, and said, How glorious was the king of Israel to day, who uncovered himself to day in the eyes of the handmaids of his servants, as one of the vain fellows shamelessly uncovereth himself!"* I think Michal's reference to "handmaids" is a thinly veiled comment about David's well-known and often uncontrolled sexuality. As a woman, I can see her anger emanating more from hurt and public humiliation than status and pride of place. She was a woman used first by her father and then by her husband and she never had children so she had no one to "arise and call her blessed". I'm not making excuses, I'm just sayin...

But back to Proverbs 31:29, *"Many daughters have done virtuously, but thou excellest them all"*. This is part of the actualization of that genuine and well-earned praise women seek. Those are sincere words pondered and well considered, rather than impulsive statements uttered for effect. <u>Barnes' Notes on the Bible</u> describes them as words of praise a husband addresses to an ideal wife. The Hebrew word for virtuously "chayil (khah'-yil)" connotes strength, force, means and resources and in this context I think it references strength of character. In <u>Clarke's Commentary on the Bible</u> we see reference to the testimony of the husband about the excellency of his wife and in fact it goes beyond merely extolling her virtue in a vacuum. This husband compares and contrasts his wife to other women-with specificity. He acknowledges daughters, other wives, mistresses and even mothers and concludes "but Thou hast ascended above the whole of them – thou hast carried every duty, every virtue, and every qualification and excellency, to a higher perfection, than any of whom we have ever read or heard". I think there are three lessons in this husband's testimony: (1) a lesson about speaking things into existence; (2) a lesson about the power of life and death in the tongue; and (3) a lesson about the domino effect of being out of order.

Let's start with the lesson about speaking things into existence. This referenced husband extols his wife, not just for what she is at any moment in time, but for what she is in the process of becoming, and by doing so he increases the likelihood that what he has spoken about her will come to pass. This praise is not just kinder, strategically it's better and more effective than what we commonly witness; husbands disparaging their wives in comparison to their mothers, their daughters or other women. My father always says he has one "First Lady"– his wife, my mother. By the same token my husband views me as his "First Lady" and just as I place no one above him, he places no one above me. Often when I'm knee-deep in multi-tasking, he'll look at me and quote the title to that old George Jones song, "What My Woman Can't Do Can't Be Done". If men in the secular world, ala George Jones, understand the value of speaking things into existence, i.e., praising a woman for what she is becoming, then surely men filled with the Holy Ghost should "get it".

That lesson is inextricably tied to the second lesson in this scripture, namely the power of death and life in the tongue. None of us as women hold ourselves out as perfect or "having attained"-at least none of us in our right minds! We frequently remind ourselves and others that "God is not through with us yet". But, admitted imperfections notwithstanding, there is a quintessential question facing the believer that asks "Whose report will you believe?" The Old Testament story of Joshua and Caleb spying out the land is an excellent example of this. "*We came unto the land whither thou sentest us, and surely it floweth with milk and honey; and this is the fruit of it. Nevertheless the people be strong that dwell in the land, and the cities are walled, and very great: and moreover we saw the children of Anak there.*" Numbers 13:27-28.

The diunital message that "yes" the land is full of milk and honey and "yes" there are big, violent folks living in it required an answer to that question "Whose report will you believe?" How does that question apply to spousal relationships? Quite simply, what position do you want to take, one of positive, flexible, confident optimism or one of rigid negativity? Will you view your spouse broadly as one steeped in the potential of becoming or narrowly as one stuck in the imperfection of any given moment in time?

The third lesson in this husband's testimony lies in the domino effect of people being out of order. This husband, by placing his wife first and behaving biblically, removes the emotional burden of caring for his wife from his children. When men are out of order, when they have children with women to whom they are not married, when they leave or divorce the mothers of their children, when they are emotionally absent and do not provide holistic support for the mothers of their children, they leave their children, especially their sons, in the precarious position of trying to fulfill a role for which they are ill suited. How often have we heard a single mother or a mother with a distant or irresponsible husband refer to her young son, not as child but as a "little man"? And how often have we heard those children, grown into men, go on, and on, and on, and on about their "Mamas"? Sadly, in most instances those men are still attempting to fulfill the role of their fathers in providing for the emotional needs of their mothers. This is one of the domino effects of being out of order.

When the husband/father is out of order, whether physically absent or emotionally distant, the child, in attempting to fill the void, is placed out of order. Conversely, when men uphold, praise and exalt their wives and the mothers of their children in accordance with Proverbs 31:29 their sons are free to love their mothers appropriately and then mature and form marital bonds of their own. In those instances their wives, rather than their mothers, are free to become their paragons of virtue–their "First Lady."

This is a gift not just to the wife/mother, it is a multi-generational gift begun with the child. When our youngest son was born, Charles gave me a small batik banner that read, "The greatest gift a father can give his children is to love their mother." It's not scriptural, but it is true. By loving me, Charles has removed any emotional, psychological or financial burden our sons might otherwise have for me. They are free to form appropriate "pair bonds" of their own that are separate and apart from me. They are able to live out the scriptural mandate outlined both the Old and New Testament. Genesis 2:24, "*Therefore shall a man leave his father and his mother, and shall cleave unto his wife: and they shall be one flesh.*" This mandate is repeated and confirmed in Ephesians 5:31 "*For this reason a man will leave his father and mother and be united to his wife, and the two will become one flesh.*"

As we come to the end of this chapter we see the echo of the praise uttered in Proverbs 31: 10, "*Who can find a virtuous woman? for her price is far above rubies.*" Proverbs 31:30 clarifies the reason or rationale for the praise by taking the comparative analysis beyond that of rubies, gems and jewels. "*Favour is deceitful, and beauty is vain: but a woman that feareth the LORD, she shall be praised."* Variations on this theme are familiar and plentiful. "Pretty is as pretty does;" "Beauty's only skin deep;" and those ominous lyrics made famous by the late, great Jimmy Soul about the connection between unhappiness and a pretty wife. But in point of fact, the outward appearance is just that, an outward appearance. Granted most of us want to look our best, even if we disagree on how to define "the best". For some, "the best" is our natural, clean, freshly scrubbed and neatly groomed selves; for many "the best" includes a bit of enhancement provided by various purveyors of beauty; and for others "the best" requires injections, scalpels, and augmentation. Regardless of how we define "the best" (or allow others to define it for us) the outward appearance has no bearing on the virtue discussed and defined in Proverbs 31.

The outward appearance is inherently fleeting, diminished and obscured by many factors: aging, illness, environmental degradation caused by free radicals and too much sun exposure, etc. But long before we knew about the necessity of sunscreen, the temporal nature of physical beauty was widely known. "Forma bonum fragile est" translates "beauty is a fragile good, a transitory blessing" or "a beautiful form is fragile". These words of wisdom were penned by Ovid (Publius Ovidius Naso, 20 March 43 BC – AD 17/18) the Roman poet, who along with Virgil and Horace is considered to be one of the three canonic poets of Latin literature and therefore of Western literature; so "this ain't no yesterday thing".

Physical beauty is a wonderful thing, it's a blessing, i.e., a favor or gift bestowed by God, but far too often we place unwise and unwarranted emphasis on it. History is replete with examples of the dangerous lure of physical beauty. Helen of Troy (formerly of Sparta), known as "the face that launched a thousand ships" was so beautiful that Paris, Prince of Troy, abducted her from her Greek husband, Meneleus, thus launching the 10 year Trojan war. Our inappropriate focus on physical beauty continues in this 21st century partly because we continue to justify and sanction that focus. We obsess about weight ("Girl, please don't let me get that big!"); proportion ("OMG! Did you see her behind, her thighs, her arms, her stomach…?!"); color ("If you're white, you're right, if you're yellow you're mellow, if you're brown stick around but if you're black-get back!" and sadly, no we're not "all passed that") and then of course there's the whole issue of hair-texture, thickness, length and shine ("Oooooo, she got some good hair!").

Sometimes we try to camouflage the shallowness of our interests by quoting famous lines of poetry-often out of context. John Keats' "Endymion", published in 1818, begins with the well-known line "A thing of beauty is a joy forever". The poem, based on the Greek myth of Endymion, a shepherd beloved by the moon goddess Selene, is as much about the beauty of nature as it is about the "love" between a human and a mythological deity. "Endymion" is an epic, i.e., very long poem, written in rhyming couplets in iambic pentameter (aka heroic couplets), but just reading the first stanza is enough to reveal the true focus.

> *"A thing of beauty is a joy for ever:*
> *Its loveliness increases; it will never*
> *Pass into nothingness; but still will keep*
> *A bower quiet for us, and a sleep*
> *Full of sweet dreams, and health, and quiet breathing.*
> *Therefore, on every morrow, are we wreathing*
> *A flowery band to bind us to the earth,*
> *Spite of despondence, of the inhuman dearth*
> *Of noble natures, of the gloomy days,*
> *Of all the unhealthy and o'er-darkened ways*
> *Made for our searching: yes, in spite of all,*
> *Some shape of beauty moves away the pall*

From our dark spirits. Such the sun, the moon,
Trees old, and young, sprouting a shady boon
For simple sheep; and such are daffodils
With the green world they live in; and clear rills
That for themselves a cooling covert make
'Gainst the hot season; the mid-forest brake,

Rich with a sprinkling of fair musk-rose blooms:
And such too is the grandeur of the dooms
We have imagined for the mighty dead;
All lovely tales that we have heard or read:
An endless fountain of immortal drink,
Pouring unto us from the heaven's brink."

The varied interpretations of epic poems notwithstanding, we know for a fact that no physical thing, beautiful or not, will last forever, nor will any joy that it imparts. But this incorrect and dangerous focus on the external is not just a weight that women carry about ourselves and one another. It also obscures and clouds our view of men. The whole idea that a man can't "step to me" unless he meets certain criteria, is deeply flawed when those criteria are all external. It's not that I think too many women have standards that are too high; I think too many of those high standards reference things that are stupid and shallow. And oddly, the highest and most inflexible standards often are held by women who could not withstand an equivalent level of externally based scrutiny.

Let's just review the first segment of Proverbs 31:30, "*Favour is deceitful, and beauty is vain…*" This does not appear to be a conditional statement, e.g., not some, not most, not often, not occasionally, but all favour is deceitful at all times. What does that mean? Whether it is the favour of a beautiful or handsome countenance, the favour of intellectual giftedness, the favour of academic achievement, the favour of solid employment or the favour of great wealth-all of it is deceitful, meaning it has no possibility of eternal endurance. Like the vanity of beauty, favour is the "sinking sands of relationships". Yet, how often do we hear even saved women expound upon the list of characteristics of potential spouses that are generally deceitful and vain. He gotta look a certain way (he can't be too short, too fat or too ugly); he gotta have the right credentials (he can't be uneducated, under-educated, unemployed or under-employed)-or, and he gotta be able to support me! Now this begs two questions, (1) why would a man meeting all those credentials and qualifications need a wife, someone scripturally defined as a "Help meet"? and (2) should such a man feel the need for a helpmeet-say to host official state dinners or something-what is the likelihood that he would select any of the aforementioned women?

I recently met a very successful businessman, Ari Weinzweig, co-founder of Zingerman's Community of Businesses, a $35+million dollar enterprise, including Zingerman's Delicatessen, Zingerman's Creamery, Zingerman's Bakehouse, and ZingTrain. He's also the author of <u>Zingerman's Guide to Good Eating</u>, <u>Zingerman's Guide to Giving Good Service</u> and <u>A Lapsed Anarchist's Approach to Building a Great Business</u>, named one of Inc. Magazine's 2010 best books for business owners. In his talk he stressed his employment/selection policy "always hire for attitude-you can teach skills!" It's not biblical, but it's applicable. Men and women both need to become much more mindful and prayerful about attitude rather than skills or accomplishments-this is a key component of Bathsheba's message to her son Solomon.

Successful unions are based upon a foundation of love and commitment, and not just to one another individually. Successful unions are based upon a foundation of love and commitment to God, to the marital relationship and to the family formed by it. Beauty fades, weight is gained, hair is lost, jobs are eliminated, wealth is diminished and economies collapse. Proverbs 31:30, "*Favour is deceitful, and beauty is vain: but a woman that feareth the LORD, she shall be praised.*" We know that the fear of the Lord is the beginning of wisdom and wisdom is what allows people to move through one set of challenges to another, perceiving and discerning what is needful in each situation. Psalms 111:10, "*The fear of the LORD is the beginning of wisdom: a good understanding have all they that do his commandments: his praise endureth for ever.*" This source of worthy praise required in the second segment of Proverbs 31:30, "*she shall be praised*" is clarified in <u>Clarke's Commentary on the Bible</u>, "...possesses true religion, ...grace that harmonizes the soul,...purifies and refines all the tempers and passions, and that ornament of beauty, a meek and quiet mind, which in the sight of God is of great price".

This concept of a meek and quiet mind as a quintessential ornament of beauty disavows the prevailing norm of depression in all its myriad forms. Further a meek and quiet mind is the manifestation of the oft-quoted but too rarely revealed, 2 Timothy 1:7, "*For God hath not given us the spirit of fear; but of power, and of love, and of a sound mind*". A meek and quiet mind is a sound mind, fully aware of the power and love that transcends and overcomes whatever elements of fear may enter our consciousness. That's part of what a wife/helpmeet does, she looks beyond the constancy of change, a challenging reality of our capitalist system and knows that God is able. And because she is a helpmeet, she helps by reassuring her husband when he becomes burdened with what "appears".

The story presented in 2 Kings 6:15-17 is instructive to us because Elisha prays not for intercession but for the vision that intercession had already occurred. "*And when the servant of the man of God was risen early, and gone forth, behold, an host compassed the city both with horses and chariots. And his servant said unto him, Alas, my master! how shall we do? And he answered, Fear not: for they that be with us are more than they that*" *be with them. And Elisha prayed, and said, LORD, I pray thee, open his eyes, that he may see. And the LORD opened the eyes of the young man; and he saw: and, behold, the mountain was full of horses and chariots of fire round about Elisha."* While this is a different context, the concept of helping to see and understand vision and intersession perfected is as critical in the role of a helpmeet as it is the role of a prophet. That's why the conclusion in Proverbs 31:31 is so appropriate in its finality *"Give her of the fruit of her hands; and let her own works praise her in the gates."*

CHAPTER 10 QUESTIONS

1. Proverbs 31:28 states *"Her children arise up, and call her blessed; her husband also, and he praiseth her."* Do you expect this from your children and husband? Have you experienced it yet? Do you think it will happen before your "Home-going"?

    _____

    _____

    _____

2. While waiting for recognition, how might you deal with the admonition in Galatians 6:9 *"And let us not be weary in well doing: for in due season we shall reap, if we faint not."*?

    _____

    _____

    _____

3. What does sincere rather than public, performance art praise look like to you?

    _____

    _____

    _____

4. Proverbs 31:29 states *"Many daughters have done virtuously, but thou excellest them all."* What do you think of this comparative praise? Should husbands see their wives (as opposed to their mothers, daughters or other women) as having "excellest them all"?

    _____

    _____

    _____

5.   What possible impact does a husband's lack of praise and recognition of his wife have on their children?

_____

_____

_____

6.   How are the dual commands of the Old Testament, Genesis 2:24 *"Therefore shall a man leave his father and his mother, and shall cleave unto his wife: and they shall be one flesh"* and the New Testament, Ephesians 5:31 *"For this cause shall a man leave his father and mother, and shall be joined unto his wife, and they two shall be one flesh"* complicated when sons see their father's absent praise? Has the increasing phenomenon of unmarried fathers contributed at least partly to the increase of "Mama's boys", e.g., grown men who constantly reference their "Mama" as the most important person in their lives?

_____

_____

_____

7.   Proverbs 31:30 reads in part *"Favour is deceitful, and beauty is vain:…"* What does this mean? If favour is deceitful, why do we seek it? If beauty is vain, why do we spend so much time and money trying to achieve it? Bottom line-Do we really believe this?

_____

_____

_____

8.   The rest of the verse states "but a woman that feareth the LORD, she shall be praised." How does this reconcile with 2 Timothy 1:7 *"For God hath not given us the spirit of fear; but of*

power, and of love, and of a sound mind."*? What are the different kinds of fear we deal with and which ones are appropriate?

_____

_____

_____

9.   How does this "sound mind" concept merge with the growing rise in clinical depression and alienation? Does the ongoing economic crisis facing many families make it more difficult to hold on to a sound mind? How might women help their husbands and children hold on to a sound mind in the midst of global economic decline?

_____

_____

_____

10. Proverbs 31:31 states *"Give her of the fruit of her hands; and let her own works praise her in the gates."* What is the "fruit of her hands"? How does it compare or contrast with the "fruit of the Spirit" identified in Galatians 5:22-23, *"… the fruit of the Spirit is love, joy, peace, longsuffering, gentleness, goodness, faith, meekness, temperance…"*?

_____

_____

_____

www.ingramcontent.com/pod-product-compliance
Lightning Source LLC
Chambersburg PA
CBHW060922040426
42445CB00011B/752

* 9 7 8 0 6 1 5 6 1 0 7 4 0 *